He Read My Letter

Sarah K.

CROSSBOOKS
PUBLISHING

CrossBooks™
A Division of LifeWay
1663 Liberty Drive
Bloomington, IN 47403
www.crossbooks.com
Phone: 1-866-879-0502

First published by CrossBooks 9/20/2010

ISBN: 978-1-6150-7277-4 (sc)
ISBN: 978-1-6150-7278-1 (hc)

Library of Congress Control Number: 2010909092

Printed in the United States of America

This book is printed on acid-free paper.

I was born in Iran to an average Muslim family. The city I was born in housed the temple of a highly regarded Muslim. Some people of that city were more religious than others. My father worked at the Muslim temple. Even in this religious atmosphere, my father fell prey to drug addiction, trying to ease the stress of his life. I am one of eight children, the fifth born. My father's drug addiction put a great strain on our average income. Aside from his addiction, he was a good-hearted man, who meant well and tried to make life nice for all of us. My mother was devoted to him and gave her all to give us the best she could.

When I was six or seven years of age, I was molested by an older man in the neighborhood. At that time, I didn't know how deeply this event would touch my life. For many years I wondered why I didn't confide in my father about this tragic violation of my childhood, for he and I had a very close relationship.

I remember preparing for my first day of school. My father surprised me with a new pair of school shoes. He and I often spent time one on one. I was very excited that my father bought me a pair of shoes that had a small heel on them. I didn't have any problem finding them the morning I started first grade, because they were with me while I slept. Although my father's sickness brought me much pain, it also gave me the opportunity to spend many hours with him, as he was on disability. My mother was busy preparing food for the family, six children still in the home, with my older sister helping her. I was at the perfect age to simply sit with my father and listen to the stories of his youth. I felt favored by the special time we spent together. I remember asking him as I listened to his teenage love stories, "Dad, when I grow up, can I marry whoever I want? Will you say no if you don't like him?" His answer was always the same: "No. It does not matter who he is; if you love him, I also will accept him." Even at this tender age of seven, I was already carried away with the dream of true love and how it would one day come for me. My father was a romantic at heart, and I was instinctively drawn to the images he described. I'm sure it was evident, for Cinderella was my favorite storybook character. Playtime would be cut short if my cousins would not permit me to be Cinderella during make-believe.

Afternoon was my time with Father because I would get home from school at noon. The elementary children in Iran attend school from eight until twelve. Often my friends would invite me to join them outside to play. Something about my father's eyes captured my heart. As I looked at him propped on one arm, lying on his mat, I instinctively realized that he was lonely and could use some company. The times I chose my father's company over that of the other children continue to warm my heart.

Mom was busy with household chores, and I was the poster child for Daddy's girl. So for the next four years of my life, I could always be found on his lap or close by.

I see now as an adult how important time spent with your child is. None of us knows what tomorrow holds, and the time we pour into our children is never wasted. Neither Dad nor I knew that our time was so limited. We simply lived in the moment. I cherish every one of those moments.

At that same time, my father became ill. Within the year, we found out it was cancer. When I was nine years old, my father died at the age of fifty-two. The loss was my first experience with heartbreak. For many years, I couldn't accept the loss of my father, and tears were my daily companion. My father's death left my forty-two-year-old mother a widow with eight children, six still in the home, the youngest of whom was only two years old. Although I didn't have long conversations with my mother, there were two pieces of advice that she made very clear to me: "God is Mighty—He will provide" and "Whenever someone shares their heart with you in confidence, put the information in your heart under lock and key and toss the key."

My mother put her whole heart into what she did for her family. Never did I hear her utter a bad word. Never did my mother smack us. She was a very devout woman. Material things held no attraction for her. Daily prayers were a priority, and she tried to instill this in her children, sometimes with the opposition of my father. Father considered a good rest as important for his young children as Mother did their devotion to prayer. My mother did what she could with my father's pension and a strong belief that God would provide.

Outwardly, I was a lively, energetic child, but inwardly, the tragedy of my father's death and the confusion of loss of innocence were two wounds that continued to bleed.

In the spring of my thirteenth year, I came home from school and found that my mother had guests. My aunt and a man I had never met were visiting with my mom. I said hello and didn't think much of it. Little did I know, my life was about to be altered forever by a three-hour visit. At that time, it was not unusual in Iran for a family to decide whom their daughter would marry, although I never expected to be one of the girls who had a husband chosen for her.

The day after my aunt's visit, I came home from school as usual. I was shocked to hear the news that my mother had promised me to this stranger. I was to be his wife. My mind was reeling; I asked her if she was kidding, but it was definitely no joke. I had always thought that one day I would marry, but not like this. My plan included two people who mutually loved one another. I explained to my mother that I did not love this man. How could I? I didn't even know him. I didn't even like him. My mom came back with the explanation that many marriages that begin with love still end up in divorce. This is a good man; love will come.

So began our betrothal. I was thirteen years old and he was twenty-four. Age might have been a stretch, but my heart was even further. I did not love him. For the next year, I cried daily. Ali, my fiancé, who was an officer in the military, would come to visit. I acted like he wasn't there. I would find some task to occupy myself with, homework and housework, anything to avoid spending time with him. I didn't want to marry him, and I tried to make that fact apparent.

One week after the engagement, our families got together to choose a ring, a time that many young girls dream about. For me, it was another part of the nightmare. I didn't try to hide my disgust with this idea of marriage. As the jewelry clerk presented different rings to me, I showed no reaction one way or the other. Finally, he chose one for me to put on. I was doing my best to show him that I didn't care about rings. In the end, it was the clerk who chose the ring. He offered his congratulations and best wishes for our future life. I gave him the coldest look I could and said, "Thank you, but he'll be back in the near future for another girl." The clerk looked a little shocked, but I wanted him to know, I wanted them all to know, "I'm not going to marry this man!"

Ali continued his visits. I reasoned to myself, *Surely if he just understood that I'm not interested, he will move on to another more willing prospect.* Of course, Mother was always close by, as was customary when a young man was calling, so I couldn't freely express my feelings. One day I had my chance. Ali showed up when Mother was away. He stood at the door, knowing better than to enter the house without proper supervision, but nonetheless, I saw my chance to make my true feelings known to him. *Surely if he heard it outright,* I reasoned, *things would change and I would return to living my teenage life.* I told him that I wanted to be completely honest with him. "Do you know that they are forcing me to marry you?" I explained. "I did not want to marry," I told him. I had plans to study. I told him that I didn't love him and that I didn't even like him. Ah, the truth was finally out. There it was, plain and bold.

His response was another shock to me. He said that he didn't mind if I wanted to study; he would let me. But to the fact that I didn't love him, didn't even like him, his response was, "I don't care if you like me or not; I like you." On that note, he left.

The marriage preparation continued. Prior to this conversation, I figured that he would not want to continue making plans for our marriage; I figured that he would demand his ring back, which I would gladly give. His response was unthinkable to me. What kind of person would want to marry a girl who declares such things to him? Now it was no longer a matter of the family forcing him on me; he was forcing himself. This new revelation brought with it new feelings of hatred. It was obvious that my feelings were of no importance to him.

Who's to say what could have happened had he simply shown regard for my feelings at this stage of our relationship? I've often wondered. I was a teenager; my heart might have been won, had he followed some simple rules of love. Love must grow. Love needs to be given, not taken. This act of control and insensitivity only sent the seeds of hatred deeper.

For the year of our engagement. Ali would visit once a week. He didn't seem fazed by my indifference to him. I continued to ignore him; he would then visit with my mom. He seemed the image of patience. But soon after the wedding, the truth came out. The patient façade was over. The true colors were now revealed.

In my mind, the fight was over. All my efforts to stop the marriage had failed. Now I would concede to the fact that Ali was my husband. I figured that I would do my best to be a good wife. But it seemed that he was constantly looking for a fight. The image of patience was nothing but a mask covering an angry man looking to pay me back for a year of the cold shoulder. Once again, I didn't understand his reaction; he was fully aware of my feelings about the marriage. If he wanted to do something about that, it seemed he had missed his opportunity. The logical thing to do if someone declares that they don't want to spend their life with you is to leave them, leave them alone. But he decided to make a covenant with me for life together. Why be angry at your own decision? But he was. It made no sense to me. Now was the time to work on getting along, but instead, all the rage poured out. From the very beginning of the marriage, we had many problems. Emotional abuse led straight to physical abuse.

My mom could see how unhappy I was, but that's not all she could see. My arms and face, filled with bruises, told the story. She felt betrayed. She trusted this man with my life that he would care for me and treat me as she and my father always had, with love and compassion. She felt that she'd been cheated. As he visited our home week after week during the year of betrothal, Ali's portrayal of himself was nothing but a mask, a fake, a phony. I felt bad for myself, but I also felt bad for my mother. I know she wanted nothing but the best for me. She kept asking me to forgive her, and I did. She had been tricked; I did not blame her. I did my best to hide from her the evidence of the abuse I was experiencing; it tortured her almost as much as it did me.

After nine months of marriage, I gave birth to a beautiful son, and I was very happy to have him. I was fourteen. Those nine months were filled with changes. Day by day, my feelings for Ali turned to fear. Instead of growing together, I was shutting down. By law, I was his wife; my body resided in his home, but I felt only one thing for him—fear.

After the birth of our first son, we moved to Jahrom. This city was approximately fifteen hours by car from my home city. Ali fixed it so that we would share a home with another couple, also newly married. The man was a friend of Ali's from work.

One day, my son was very sick. The same day, our friends had company; the man's sister came to visit with them. The couple and the sister went out to shop and eat, and Ali went with them, while I stayed home with the baby. Early evening turned into late evening. I sat outside on the porch, waiting for Ali. My fears were compounding. I was afraid for my son; I didn't know what to do for him. I was afraid to be home alone in the evening. I was all right until about 8:00 PM; Ali knew this.

Our house was situated by a densely wooded area; God only knew who could be hiding in there. To sit in the house and hear strange noises was more than I could bear. My fears were all ganging up on me in this city so far from home. I planted myself on the front porch and simply waited. At about 11:00 PM, they came home. I said to Ali, "You know your child is sick; you know I'm afraid to be at home alone late at night. Why are you so late?"

He pushed me, along with our baby, into our room, locked the door, and began to beat me. He beat me so much that his friend came to our door and threatened to break it down if he did not stop. When, at last, he finished with me, I was unconscious. His friend insisted he take me to the hospital. On the way there, I was instructed to say I fell. Ali told me he would kill me if I told the doctor that my injuries were from him. My bruised and broken arm, along with my swollen face, was a dead giveaway. The doctor questioned me many times about my husband. I believed Ali's threats, so I dutifully told the story. "I fell down the steps."

Life with Ali was so difficult, I decided to divorce him. His response to my decision was to take my son from me. Knowing the way he treated me—and even in such a short time, the way he treated his own son—made that option an impossibility for me. I would never leave my child with this man. Divorce was no longer a possibility either. In Iran, no court would take up my cause, for the law says that a woman divorcing her husband can only keep her son until he is two years old. For girls, it's a little different:

she can stay with her mother until she is seven years old but then must return to her father also. This is the law. The father is in control and can do what he wants concerning his children.

In the next four years, I had two more wonderful and beautiful sons. Aside from my love for God, I loved my children more than anything. The passing years only increased my problems. Each day I feared his arrival from work. I began going to a psychiatrist to deal with my depression. He prescribed some pills to help me relax.

The abuse continued. There were times when I was injured so badly that surgery was required. My gall bladder had to be removed after a severe kick. My shoulder was so damaged that it required surgery later. A broken arm was one of my many injuries. Then there were the times he tried to kill me. Once he came at me with a knife, and another time he tried to push me in the drain hole that was being worked on in the house.

My mom had surgery on her eyes when my son Alex was three. I asked my husband if I could go visit her in the hospital. He knew my mom was everything to me. He said, "I'm not going to take you, but you can go." I was very happy and hurried to dress and cover up for the trip out of my prison. But as I prepared to leave, he turned to me and said, "Nope, you're not going."

"Why?" I asked him. "If you don't want me to go out by myself, you can take me. Please. You said I could go!"

At that moment, his face changed to someone else's entirely. His rage took over his body, and he grabbed our largest kitchen knife, lunged at me, grabbed me, and pulled back his arm, ready to give the final blow. In this short moment, I saw my three-year-old son watching with terror in his eyes at the evil rage possessing his dad. I didn't know how, but the next thing I knew, I had slipped out of his grasp and was fleeing the house bareheaded and screaming out to the street. A neighbor lady heard me. This was a miracle. I collapsed into her doorway in a total state of shock and stayed there. As she tended to my panic, she called my brother to come. She even gave me a shot of medication to calm my state of shock; she was a nurse by trade. My retreat didn't last. Within twenty-four hours, I was back in my husband's home.

He justified his actions only in front of my brothers and my mom. But to me he never said a word except for more threats and more curses on my life.

One day I packed up my boys and fled to Mom's house. He didn't follow me. I felt surely he would forget about us, but within three days he came for his "property"—the boys and me. I sat in shock as he grabbed them like sheep for the slaughter and boldly threw these little guys into the car as they screamed at the top of their lungs for me. My gut instinct took over as I ran toward him, only to be stopped by a swift kick to the gut by his steel-toed military boot. I fell into unconsciousness as he drove away with my only reason to keep living, my precious sons.

Over the next two and a half months, I lay in my mother's house. I cried a lot. I hurt physically. My husband had taken the boys to a house out of town, and he had no intention of reuniting us until I returned to the prison he called our home.

As I lie in my mother's house, I overheard stories of my husband's unfaithfulness. *Why does he keep me like this?* I asked God. No reply.

I couldn't eat. I couldn't talk. Life was over for me. It was then that I made my decision: if I die, I die beside my sons.

After ninety days, I moved home and celebrated my homecoming with gall bladder surgery to remove the crushed organ from my ravaged body. That was one deadly boot.

As I healed from surgery, I remembered my childhood dream: I wanted to be an astronaut. I would look into the stars and plan my future. It was going to be awesome. I felt loved and confident, like there was nothing I couldn't do. Again, it was just how God made me and how I thrived under my father's and family's love. At my wedding, I felt my dreams slip away as the wedding ring that became my ball and chain was slipped onto my hand—as if to cement this ending of my dreams. A cousin teased as I left the ceremony,

"Here comes the astronaut-Ha-Not!"

Plan B began as I asked my husband for permission to study. My crazy astronaut dream was not to be, but I couldn't put out the fire and hope in my spirit. I wanted to do something, be something. Again, I asked. I began to learn the game. Permission was granted, but there was no assurance that my books wouldn't be thrown out. I learned to study in secret. I often did my homework while locked in the bathroom. As I started excelling, he shut me down, saying, "You will never leave to work."

Okay, plan C: I got my hairstylist license, telling him I would work out of our home only with women, as Iranian law required. I would also be giving him 100 percent of my income. I don't know why, but I never gave up on my big dream of reaching the stars, but I put it away in a safe place as I struggled to make a place for myself to hold on to the hope—the astronaut in waiting.

Life continued on, with the verbal abuse, the beating, the unfaithfulness, and the prison. I remember that when he would curse me and torment me, I had a secret game I would play. I would hide my hand and move my finger, just one little finger, and I would say in my head, "I am free. I am free." That little finger was free. It was a source of hope to me; as each new injury was given, I would hope. Maybe this time the court will help me. They will let me leave him. There was no way. Iranian law was firm; the children are the man's property. Honestly, my only hope in this world was God, my sons, and my mom. I loved them so much. I still loved God. I still believed in marriage. I was a faithful wife. It's just who I was. I wasn't a saint, just a woman.

As I battled to make sense of the disaster that was my daily life, I found that I was pregnant again. I just knew; no pregnancy test was needed. This would not be happy news for the expectant father, just dread and unspeakable hopelessness.

After finding out about this new development, I said not a word to Ali. There was nothing to say. I hadn't even accepted the reality of the situation. To top off this week, we had another fight—one of our many. This time I couldn't stay; I told him I wanted a divorce, and he disregarded this as always. I went to my mom's house for a few days. I couldn't take the stress. I couldn't tell him I was pregnant.

My auntie was there with my mom. I told them everything—the fighting, the pregnancy. I told them I didn't want to have this baby. I wanted to have an abortion. They pleaded with me. "No, this could be the baby that changes things in your marriage," they would say. But I knew I had three kids and they had not saved my marriage. They knew my children were my dearest source of joy, but at that moment, I came to a decision. I would not have four children. I never let my mind go to the baby that was inside of me. I just stayed in survival mode. *I will not go through this pregnancy; I cannot.*

As this time in Iran, law stated that abortions were illegal. My cousin told me about how to get the abortion on the black market, but it cost a lot of money. I had the address of a place that didn't charge much. It wasn't a nice place, but I still decided to go there.

I walked in and met the receptionist, who had no personality and had the appearance of a cold stone wall. I sat in that second-floor waiting room and heard the screams coming from the next room. I was terrified. I asked the receptionist, "Why all the screaming?"

She said, "Why do you think? For this low price you don't get any painkiller—just pain." I sat frozen in my seat and waited.

Finally, the doctor came in and approached me with the question, "Do you want an abortion? Are you next?"

I started saying that I had my three sons and my husband was very abusive to us and I just couldn't go through with this pregnancy.

He looked in my eyes as I was explaining and reached out and touched my face—a mole on my cheek—and said, "Oh, is this real?" My skin began to crawl. What would he do to me in that room? Was there more to the abortion than just the torturous pain of the procedure? Was he part of the torture too?

Quickly I made up a story that I was just here to get information today and I would return tomorrow for the abortion. I hurried out of that horrible homemade clinic.

Later I learned he was a mortician by trade. He did abortions for extra cash. A friend told me about a woman who had just had an abortion. She went home and died within days. Her uterus had been punctured many times and they couldn't save her life. I still had to get out of this pregnancy, so I borrowed the money from my cousin for the expensive abortion that was impossible in Iran. I went to the doctor's "private clinic." He was an OB-GYN. I went to his office and gave him the money, and he gave me a shot that would cause me a bit of bleeding. This would illegally allow me to enter the hospital as a legitimate patient. He told me to come to the hospital the next day. "But ... and this is important," he said, "be sure to bring urine from someone who is not pregnant."

The next morning, the spotting came as promised. I had my secret urine sample I had gotten from one of the boys, and I entered the hospital with symptoms of "having a miscarriage."

They told me to go into the bathroom and bring out a urine sample as the nurse waited outside the door for me. I switched my pregnancy urine for the non-pregnancy sample and handed it to the nurse. The diagnosis was miscarriage, and I was sent to surgery for a D&C procedure to clear out my uterus. This was allowed in Iran, but abortions were not. Then my expensive doctor came in and gave me what I wanted, an end to my pregnancy—the thing that was impossible in Iran.

The abortion was finished. I was unconscious in the recovery room, or so I thought. As I opened my eyes, I saw myself above me, looking down on my body, watching the doctors and nurses huddled around me. At that moment, I was sure I was gone. I said, "I want to go to God." As I said these words, I was suddenly back in my body, lying on the hospital bed as the doctors were slapping the side of my face, which was wet with tears.

Later, they told me, "Wow, you were gone for a moment—no breathing, no heartbeat. We had to restart your heart with CPR. Then suddenly you were back to life. You were crying and saying, 'I want to go to God.'" I never forgot that amazing moment.

Another interesting thing was that the very day I was ending my pregnancy, my husband was searching every hospital in town for me. He had heard about the pregnancy and was determined to find me. God alone knows how he missed the one hospital I was in. When he came to get me at my mom's house, I had to keep my face like flint. I had to tell him that he was mistaken. There never had been a pregnancy, and certainly not an abortion. That was impossible in Iran, anyway.

He took us home, and I carried this most painful secret in my heart. I had taken the life of this baby to preserve the life of my sons and me. I believe this was all I could handle, and the load was getting heavier.

If it could even be possible, life got worse. My husband's fury, along with me trying to hold my sons' lives and my life together was all the strength my twenty-three-year-old heart could generate. I was going down quickly.

I decided I could no longer go on, not for my dear mom, my precious boys, and not even for God. It was a relief. I would kill myself. *No more pain outside me or inside me. This is my plan. This is what I'm going to do.*

As I sat finalizing this last chore, a radio news program was playing in the kitchen. The lady's voice caught my ear. Her tone sounded like mine with what she was saying. Apparently, she was being interviewed after a failed suicide attempt. She had taken her children with her. As they had thrown themselves into the water, a man had seen her. He chose her. He pulled her out of death's grip while her beloved children drowned. Now she was being interviewed by this news show. They asked her what she was thinking. She said she wanted the pain to stop. She went on to describe her husband, who was like mine. She saw no other way; now all that was left was to finish the job on her.

Next came the judge's comments. He said he would press for the most punishment possible for this horrible person. There wasn't a word about what drove her to it. Her husband was next in the interview. When asked, he said, "Ha, she was crazy, that's all, just crazy." That statement changed everything for me.

She was not crazy! This I knew more than life itself. She was not crazy, and I am not crazy. I will not have my husband leaving my boys with that legacy, that inheritance: "Your mom was just crazy." So, right then and there, I changed my plan. I decided to live. As my decision to live came to life, so did my stored-up dreams. The astronaut dreamer in me came back. *I can do this! I can live! I want to live!* But I knew I didn't want to live here, not like this. My boys' lives were at the top of my mind now, and a plan started to pour into my mind: escape! Iran was not sympathetic to the pain and suffering of my sons or me. I had to leave; an impossible plan, in that a woman was required to have her husband's permission to get a visa at that time. I turned to God and renewed my faith and hope in him. If we were to escape, he would have to light the path and make each element fit perfectly with the next.

Within two days, the way started to become clear. I found out there was one place where a visa was not required: Turkey, my lifeboat. But how could I reach it? My city did not have an international airport. We would have to fly to Tehran first, and how to pay? As I sold my gold jewelry, the fear inside me became larger than life. I had never given my husband a reason to beat me. What I was doing now was beyond daring, beyond dreaming. I was a twenty-three-year-old Iranian mother with three small boys. My hope of death had now been replaced by a hope of life. It would be a different life. It would be a free life. Not just my little finger, but my sons and me. It was liftoff time. Now I was off to purchase the tickets.

As I entered the ticket office in my hometown, I can honestly say I had never to that point in my life felt such fear and pressure on my body and spirit as I did that dreaded winter day. These were the thoughts going through me: *He has never let me out of his control for a whole night. How will we get to the plane, to Turkey? What in the world will I do in Turkey? How will we live? I know no one there. How will he not find out about this, and will we make it to Tehran? How will we make it out of there? He will find us and kill us.* All of this settled upon my little twenty-three-year-old soul in a silent scream that could not be let out under any circumstances. No one could know. I had no answers to my questions, and under no circumstances could I go to anyone for help—not my mother, not family. They couldn't be a part of this sacred journey, my last-ditch effort for life. It was too much of a divine work of God that only he could be trusted with. Even in their love for me, a misspoken word to the wrong person could mean the end of my sons and me.

As I held the tickets in my hand, believing that no human could live through what I was feeling in my heart, a fear, cold and real, hit me. I turned around and came face to face with my cousin. I felt my life drain away as he said, "Sarah, what are you doing here?" I prayed to God right then and there at the ticket counter for him to allow me to melt into the hard cement floor beneath my feet. But it was not to be; instead, every fear, every passion, everything that I possessed in each cell of my body seemed to suddenly converge in my eyes as I stared into his and mouthed these words, "Please don't tell."

I looked into my cousin's eyes at the ticket office as a dead woman. God, how can one person hold this amount of terror and dread in her heart? I felt like I might be sweating blood as I heard the words come out of his mouth: "Okay, Sarah, I won't tell."

I went home to wait. Wait for the bottom to fall out, for my cousin to break his promise, for my husband to read this new level of fear on my face. As I walked around him on eggshells, the tears fell heavier than ever before. I had always stopped them quickly in the past, but now the flood came.

My boys were young, and I was about to alter their lives forever. They did not have any kind of relationship with their dad besides intimidation. I really felt a need to do this, for them and for me. At the same time, I had to tell them before they were whisked away from the only home they've ever known.

I told my little eight-, six-, and four-year-old sons what I intended to do for us and why. They listened with as much attention and seriousness as their young hearts could generate. They promised not to tell anyone. Another layer of terror settled on me.

As the two-week window of opportunity to get on our plane to freedom approached, Ali sensed my anticipation. As if a parting gift, he gave me one of the most vicious verbal attacks ever. At that point, I snapped; my spirit was crushed to a powder. But my tickets were in my possession. I did something very strange: I answered him. I looked into those cold eyes, the ones that had taken me against my will as a child, a child who could have learned to respect and even love him. But he had treated me like an animal instead of a wife. He left a legacy of fear instead of love. I said these words as the truest thing I'd ever speak: "Someday I will leave you."

Ali laughed out loud, a deep, evil, haunting laugh. "Sarah, you can never leave me!" He knew my immense fear. He knew my huge weakness of losing those three precious boys. But he didn't know me, the dreamer, the astronaut, the Sarah who was trusting God again to lead her step by step across the rickety swinging footbridge that spanned from my prison to our future. He didn't know that in my heart, I was already gone.

My heart may have been gone, but my mind was definitely still in Iran, as the hows and the what-ifs trampled through my battered mind. *How will I get permission to be gone for a whole night?* This had never happened before, outside of nights at my mom's house with him popping in or calling unannounced at all hours. *Think, Sarah, think. Flight to Tehran leaves at noon. Then a day there until 6:00 AM flight to Turkey. Where would we sleep?*

He could find me missing and with one call have me pulled from the airport back to his grasp.

This was the winter of 1989 in Iran, and the law was firm: no married woman, especially with three sons, could purchase a room in a hotel without her husband's permission. But God had laid down one more plank on the bridge to freedom. I had a phone number of an old childhood friend who had moved to Tehran. Would she help us? Did this number even work? I had never called her; *crazy, Sarah, crazy.*

As I woke in the early morning on D-day, the plan poured out of a mouth so unaccustomed to speaking to my husband. "May I have permission to take the boys and stay over at my cousin's home tonight? Her husband is gone, and she is having lady guests over."

He looked at me and said, "Yes, Sarah, you may go."

I may go. I may go! This was such a small victory, remembering the many times his *yes* turned to *no* at the last minute or he came for me unexpectedly. Also, my cousin had a phone. She knew nothing about my plan of escape; there was no ladies' party.

That morning, I set the house in as perfect order as I have ever done. I laid out his favorite foods, even the tea. I packed our single suitcase of winter clothes, for I had only two hands: one for the case and one for my bewildered boys. As we set out from our home that morning, I grabbed one loaf of bread and cheese and prayed for God to hold that bridge together just long enough for us to pass over.

I felt no let-up from the constricting fear as we boarded the plane and flew the one-hour flight to Tehran, for we were still in the land of my captor. So many miracles had to happen yet if we were to get out of Iran.

We arrived in Tehran and the next risky step on our journey. I looked down at that tattered number of my childhood neighbor, who had married a man who lived in Tehran—the one I had many years left behind with my marriage. The number I had never called. I dialed and held my breath. I heard the sound that was water to my soul: my friend's voice. I put on my false confidence mask and greeted her. I explained that I was in Tehran and asked if I may visit with her.

Within an hour, we were sitting in the home she shared with her husband, a very religious Muslim. As we spoke, I had to remind myself to breathe. *Don't show your fear, Sarah. Keep your mask on tightly.* I told my story. I was here with my husband's permission. I was going to secure a visa to visit my friend Sanaz in Sweden by way of Pakistan—because it was Eastern. That should throw my husband off our trail if he questioned my friends.

My friend looked into my eyes. *Oh, God, she knows me. She knows him. She knows I'm lying.* But as my soul silently screamed, *Help me!* I continued to answer their many questions with a calm cool. "Of course my husband permits this. Of course he has given his consent—no problem."

That night, we slept—or rather waited for morning—for our 6:00 AM flight to freedom. I can honestly say this was a night of crushing fear. *Does he know? Did my cousin call him? Will he be waiting for me at the airport? Maybe he will come here now.* At that exact minute, at 2:00 in the morning, the doorbell at my friend's home rang, and my heart exploded within my chest. *This is the end. I am a dead woman.*

But it was not to be. Again I rose from the deep as my friend's brother entered from that door, saying, "Hello, sorry I didn't call, but I just got into the city."

The night broke into morning, and the husband took us to the airport. He insisted on accompanying us to our gate. *Oh no, he cannot see where we are going!* With the last bit of air I had left in my lungs, I said, "No! No! I do not want you to," and I walked away from that car with one suitcase and my three reasons for living.

What if I'd already been found out? There were so many what-ifs. What if my husband had already discovered that I wasn't really at my cousin's house? What if they were already looking for me? What if they were prepared to arrest me when I presented the boarding pass? My mind was racing with the terror of discovery, but what if I don't try? *I will do it. I must continue.*

Although I was filled with more anxiety than I can describe, my face did not betray my feelings. I kept the exterior under control. I was simply a woman with her children, going on a trip. No one would know.

I presented my boarding passes. They received them with no problem. I was relieved, for a moment. But I quickly remembered that I was not off the ground yet. They could still come for me at any moment. Maybe that's the way it worked—let her pass and send for the police to collect her from the plane. Onward I went. I led the children to their seats, and we got settled in. Then I spotted him—a man, clearly a plainclothes security officer, I could tell by his dark glasses and his suit, searching the aisles up and down. He was looking for something, for someone. I was screaming on the inside, *this is it, this is it!*

The only move I could make was to push my back deeper into the seat. Besides that, I was numb. I was frozen, just waiting for the end to come. I looked at my children, but I couldn't speak. Then he turned around. He left the plane. Was he going to report that he'd found me? Was he speaking to them now and getting help to escort me off the plane? Still frozen, I waited. Then I heard the door close, we began to taxi to the runway. Could it be? Everything in me began to scream. A silent scream ... *Take off! Take off! Take off!*

The plane found its place on the runway and began to accelerate, faster, faster, and then finally lifted off. My spirit was one with the airplane; my entire being was lifting off along with it. I was flying; hope filled my body. For now, I was safely on my way; what I would face on the next leg of my journey, I did not know. The tears of relief began to flow. I was flying. To this day, I love the moment of liftoff.

We landed in Turkey. What next? *Get the luggage, yeah, that's it, get the luggage.* I gathered our belongings and began to wander around. I saw a security guard, and my senses heightened. He was talking on a walkie-talkie ... in Persian. Why was he talking in Persian? He should be speaking in Turkish. *Oh God, what did he say?* "The case you are looking for is here." He sees me, he's talking about me. He's reporting—in Persian—to the Persian authorities that *I* am here. Panic rose in me. I grabbed my bags, I grabbed my children's hands; I told them to hold on to one another and run.

We ran to the nearest exit and out the door. A taxi was just sitting there. I opened the door and urgently told my children to get in. The taxi driver sensed my panic and jumped out to put my suitcases in the trunk. He asked me, "Where to?" I just said "Go ... go!" He did. After we got away from the airport, he asked again "Where to?" In my extremely limited English, I said, "Hotel."

I presented myself at the desk of the hotel and asked for a room. Thank God the man did not ask me for my husband's permission. He assigned us our room, and up we went. Once behind locked doors, I took out our cheese and bread and fed my children. After our simple meal was finished, I decided I would now call my friend Sanaz in Sweden. I locked the door to the room and told my children not to open it for anyone. I went back to the man at the desk and asked him if there was a place to make a long-distance call. I couldn't call from the room, with its expensive rates, and was happy to hear that there was a station right around the corner with public phones. I found my way there and made my call.

My friend answered, and I told her I was in Turkey with my three children. I told her I had escaped from my husband and left Iran. She was in shock. She began to yell at me. "Are you crazy? A young woman with three children in Turkey! Do you even know what could happen? Oh God, what are you thinking? I can call your husband and talk to him. I'll smooth things over with him, and you can go back. You must go back."

I told her that I only called her because I trusted her. I told her I would not go back and I needed her help. She proceeded to try to convince me that I must go back. As I listened to her, all the emotions, all the stress, all the fear came together with one voice in me, and I told her, "Let me tell you again: I'm calling you because I trust you. If you do not help me, you will never hear from me again. I want you to know that if you don't help me now, my blood will be on your hands. Ali has tried to kill me many times when I've done nothing. I've been beaten nearly to death for doing nothing. Now I've left him, I've left the country. Can you imagine what he would do to me? But I'll never give him the chance, because I'll kill myself. You don't know what I've been through, really, you have no idea. It's nothing short of a miracle that I've made it this far. Truly, you can't imagine; it's been one miracle after another that I've come this far. If you could only know, you would never suggest that I turn around and go back. Believe me, I will not go back, I promise you. If you do not help me, you will never hear from me or my children again."

Finally, she heard me; she understood that I was not just mildly unhappy. She must have heard the desperation in my voice because she said, "Okay, okay."

As I lay in bed that night, looking at my children sleeping peacefully, the enormity of what I had just done started hitting me. The first wave hit me ... my mom. I had not only left Ali, I had left my precious mom. The second wave hit me ... my family. My brothers and sisters; I had left my brothers and sisters. The third wave ... my country. I had left my homeland, the place of my birth. The thoughts just kept coming. I recounted all that had happened in the last two days. I wondered what Ali would do when he received the letter I had written while I was in Tehran. In the letter, I tried to explain to him why it had come to this. I reminded him how I was only a teenager when we married and how my feelings could have grown if only he had treated me with patience, gentleness, and respect. Love could have been ours. We had children together; they are also your children, I told him. In my letter, I reminded him how I wouldn't stay forever in the abuse. Was he seriously considering my advice about how to treat the next woman in his life? I wondered what impact it had on him when he read that I was gone for good. Of course, the possibility of getting caught was still very real, and so was the fear that went with it. I tried not to think about it.

My friend in Sweden now held all my hopes in her hands. What could she do? Moreover, what if she could do nothing? The thoughts rolled in and out with my tears until sleep finally overtook me.

I spent the next six months in Turkey, waiting for the next door to open. I learned there was a man who would fix a passport for me and my children. There would be a fee; it was very expensive. We stayed in an apartment with other refugees waiting for the opportunity to escape. Those six months felt like sixty years.

In Turkey, I thought that I finally could breathe and find some peace and safety from the nightmare I had escaped. I called my friend in Sweden, who quickly informed me that my nightmare had only just begun.

My husband, being a military officer in Iran, had the power to send officials anywhere in Turkey to arrest whomever he chose. It appeared that his sources had located information that led him to know that the children and I had escaped to Turkey. He was hunting me like a wild animal.

The paralyzing fear, agonizing pain, and incredible stress engulfed me and threatened to consume me and pull me under to my death. I was terrified of every person who looked my way; every noise I heard in the night made my heart leap from my chest in terror.

My friend found that there were smugglers who were able to create fake passports and visas, and secure transportation and lodging for a fee. The price the smugglers needed to get us from Turkey to Sweden was $12,000. My friend was able to get a bank loan for $8,000, with the remaining $4,000 to be paid once we arrived.

Once I got to Sweden, I would be expected to pay off my $12,000 debt as soon as I got a job. That was the least of my worries.

My friend gave me the date, time, and location where the boys and I would meet the strangers who would now be in charge of our safe passage to Sweden. We met at the arranged place. We were put in a car and driven to an undisclosed location within Turkey. I called it the hiding place.

The hiding place was a small building with several rooms, like an apartment building, except that the tenants were people of all ages and stations of life who were all escaping danger. We were all refugees of our own private wars. The boys and I shared a small room. Other families were placed together in other rooms. Single people were often placed several to a room to save space.

I remember the nightmares I had there—they were always the same: horrible dreams of having my precious children snatched away from me. It was very painful for me as a mother. My children, who were eight, six, and four at the time, needed me to be strong. They were scared and confused, and although I would try to soothe them, I knew that when they looked in my eyes, all they saw was fear. My heart hurt that I was unable to be the security they needed so much.

Every second dragged on like a year. Time seemed to stand still. Every day ticked by until someone's name would be called. Finally, it was our turn. We were hurriedly shuffled to the airport along with several others from the hiding place. Once we got there, we were gathering our things and preparing to check in when our smugglers caught sight of the police approaching. We were quickly whisked back into the waiting car and to the apartment to await a safer time to go.

These trips to the airport happened several times, at all hours of the night and even early morning. How difficult to roust three tired children from their beds at 3:00 AM and drag them to the airport, only to be hurried back to the car when the police would be too near. The new chief of police in Turkey was very persistent with airport security at that time and was cracking down on illegal passports, so it was very difficult to find a safe time to go to the airport.

The uncertainty of knowing when we would be taken to the airport, along with fear and fatigue, was wearing heavy on my heart. But during this time, I experienced the crushing burden of some horrible secrets that I had carried with me. The shame of being molested at the age of six came back in full force when I was forcibly raped earlier in Turkey. My attempts to fight off my attacker were met with several punches to my head. Because of my situation, I could not go to the police to report this crime. I felt trapped and dirty and full of shame. My spirit felt abused and unclean. I had no one I could talk to; there was no one to hold me, protect me, or help me after this vicious attack. Silent screams of rage, anger, hurt, and frustration welled up in me. I was locked in a prison of fear and secrecy and shame.

When I began experiencing morning sickness, I realized that I was pregnant by the man who had sexually abused me. There was so much rushing and waiting and sickness and grief. I had come to the end of my rope. I could not keep up this pace. I was completely drained of life itself. There was nothing left within me, and that night, after another unsuccessful attempt to get out of Turkey, I wrote a letter to God:

> Dear God,
>
> You know all about me. You know all about my childhood … the hardship and the pain. You know about my marriage. You know about everything. God, I have no one else to talk to. I have no one with which to share this incredible pain and grief, but I know that I can share this with you.
>
> God, if I didn't think you could help me, I would never have left Iran. Yet I am so very tired, God. I am tired of all this waiting. I am weak and sick and afraid. I am a broken-down boat in the midst of a great stormy sea. I have these children, God, and they need me to protect them. They need a mother. God, I need you to help me. If you cannot hear my voice, maybe you can read my letter.
>
> From, Sarah

That very night, after I wrote that letter, the smugglers came to tell me to get the boys ready. We would be trying to leave early the very next morning. *So many trips back and forth to the airport,* I thought to myself. *I wonder if this one would be any different.*

At 4:00 AM, forty of us came out from the hiding place, got into cars, and headed once again to the airport. The air was crisp and cold as we arrived at the airport entrance. Our fears turned to hope and our hope turned to joy as we were able to go directly through the check-in, right to our gate, and straight onto our waiting plane! I could hardly contain my excitement and joy and wonder at the fact that my boys and I were actually on our way to Bulgaria! As the plane lifted off, I could feel my heart lifting shouts of praise to God.

He read my letter!

The trip from Turkey to Bulgaria was without incident. All I knew was we were getting closer to our destination. We met up with other refugees in Bulgaria. At a hotel, we were grouped with those who were to continue on to Sweden.

I felt a little relief, thinking that no one knew I was in Bulgaria. Ali couldn't reach me here. Only one more leg of the journey was left. One more plane ride and we would be safe. At night, though, the nightmares continued. I would wake up, quickly checking my boys to see if they were safe by me. The images of them being taken from me haunted my sleep. Between this disrupted sleep and the throwing up from the constant nausea, my body's endurance was being tested.

Our group boarded the plane bound for Sweden. Some new faces, some familiar, we were about forty-five in all. Things were moving fast now. The nightmare was almost over. Liftoff—my heart soared again with the plane. As we were flying, the unthinkable happened: a man in our group was recognized. Someone figured out that he was not who he claimed to be. Our cover was blown. In a short time, we were all discovered. The smuggler who was traveling with us gave instructions to be passed among us. The word traveled quickly: "Tell no one where you came from, tell no one your real name, and tell no one where you are going." We followed his instructions. We trusted him. We had no choice. After that, I never saw him again.

The plane landed. What would happen now? We were not in Sweden. We were in Norway. As we exited the plane, there were several tall Norwegian police officers who were huge and very intimidating. My heart was pounding; everyone was looking. Somehow, these officers knew exactly who to extract from the group of exiting passengers. They picked us out one by one, gathered us up, and put us in police cars. We were taken to a sort of warehouse/jail by the airport.

This airport jail consisted of long hallways with many rooms, and every room was carefully monitored by cameras. They could watch every move we made. Every window was covered with bars. Each day, one of those tall police officers would enter our halls with bread, butter, and jelly—that was it for the day.

The day after we arrived, we were taken before a judge. He asked all the questions you would expect: Where are you from? What is your name? Where are you going? We said nothing, just like our smuggler instructed us. *Could the air get any tighter?* I thought to myself. The tension was so thick, I didn't think I could breathe the air. Just to speak to my children was a source of tension—I couldn't call them by their real names. Nothing was natural. Every word required attentive thought. Even my boys, so young, having to keep such secrets. I would have liked to keep the situation light, for their sake, call it make-believe, but that was not an option. The situation was so serious that I had to emphasize the danger. "Do not call your brother by his real name." Over and over I had to scold my poor children for the simple act of saying each other's names. So many secrets, each one draining me of the little energy I had left. The officials knew this. They were counting on it. Sooner or later, someone was going to hit bottom, and when they did, the truth would come out and we would all be sent back to where we came from.

I remember one day in particular, when one of the men could bear it no longer. He found a sharp instrument and slit his wrists. We screamed; we yelled for help. "Please take him to the hospital!" we pleaded. They were not moved. They sent someone in to bind up his wrists, but he stayed right there behind those cold bars. The way the authorities viewed the situation, we had no right to put our feet in their country. They would wait until someone was ready to talk.

The days wore on, about thirty days and counting. Up in the morning, and walk the halls to the small living room. Two tables, one with water, the other with the bread and butter; that was all we could look forward to. I paced like a caged animal. My boys were suffering also. The close quarters were wearing on them too. My youngest, Alex, four years old, could see out the barred window. There was a nice area with grass and some water. One of the officers, who cared for two large black dogs, was walking them in that area. The dogs ran freely around the yard, and the man played with them so they could get their exercise.

As my youngest watched, he asked, "Mom, why can the dogs go outside to play but I can't?" and he began to cry. That question was like a dagger straight into my heart. At that point, I began to beat my fist upon the wall and scream with all my might, "When are you going to let us out? What do you have to say to a four-year-old child? The dogs are treated better than him. What can you say to him? Answer me!" I screamed and screamed.

I'm sure they figured time had done its job. One of them has cracked, they probably thought. They quickly summoned their Persian interpreter. Of course, they didn't know what I was saying, and I'm sure they hoped I was ready to tell them what they wanted to hear. I cried to the man, "How can you treat us this way? What can I tell my child? Can you please tell me? What should I tell him?" I could tell the man felt bad for me, but there was nothing he could do for me. It was not in his power to change my situation.

The cell we were being held in had cameras that were watching us around the clock, recording every word, every expression, and every outburst. I was very afraid that I would slip and call my sons by their real names. It was very difficult to keep up the charade and live under this microscope where our every move was scrutinized. The guards were hoping that the stress and hardship of being held against our will would eventually make someone crack under the pressure and spill the whole secret. They were watching for those of us who appeared to be ready to talk.

The day after my outburst with the guard, I was summoned to the interrogation room. The people in my cell were very fearful that I would spill the secret. I was very weak and broken and tired. I could no longer keep up the mask that everything was okay. I was sure that they could take one look at me and read me like a book. I felt like my soul was outside my body, like I no longer existed. But I willed myself to put one foot in front of the other as I slowly made my way to the interrogation room.

I arrived to find that this day, the chief of the whole police department would be interviewing me. I could tell by the way the other officers treated him that this was a man to be respected and feared. He sat casually across the table and leaned back as if to show me that he was in complete control. As I sat down across from him, he tried to intimidate me by slowly pulling out his hand and as if he had a gun and saying, "Bang, bang, bang."

By this time, I had no more fear of physical harm; my only fear was being sent back to Iran. I was angry and defiant as I snapped back, "Sir, I am not afraid of guns; I come from a country where children play with guns." Surprised by my boldness, he quickly sat back and proceeded to ask me question after question. Somehow, I summoned the strength to stand firm.

The guard switched on the recorder and proceeded with his questioning.

"What's your name?"

"My name is Roya." I gave him my false name, Roya, which means "vision" in Persian.

"From what country have you flown, and where did you get your false passport?"

"I am Iranian. I will not tell you what country I got my passport."

"What airport have you arrived from?"

"I'm sorry; I will not tell you."

"Why are you fleeing Iran?"

"There were problems with my husband, and I feared for our lives"

"Do you know I have the power to send you back to Iran or to give you and your children residency here in Norway?"

"Yes, sir, I realize that."

"I'm going to make this really easy for you, if you will only give me the information I need. If you will tell me what airport you came from and who got you those passports, I will promise to grant you and your children residency here. You will be free to go. You won't even have to go back to the cell. We will bring your children and we will take care of all your needs. Residency, apartment, and money; whatever you need. The others will be sent back, but I will spare you and your children if you will only cooperate with us.

After so many weeks of anguish in the small holding cell, I briefly thought for a moment about the possibility of freedom for myself and my boys. But something greater than my freedom was at stake here.

"Sir, let me tell you something: I didn't come here because you gave me food or lodging. I came to this country because I want to be free. I came here because my husband treated us as animals. I came here to get away from inhumane conditions. I don't know everyone's story, but I know that they all risked their lives to get here. We have overcome horrible things—hunger, pain, and sickness. All because we want freedom! I have risked all that I am and all that I have for this. If I were to tell you what you want to hear and send all those people back, I would not be living the type of life that I am looking for. If I don't act humanely and with justice toward others, how can I expect to be treated with dignity and humanity myself? I will not tell you another thing, no matter how many times you bring me here."

The chief stared at me for what seemed like hours and then said, "Okay, you can go."

I arrived back at the cell to the relieved cries and hugs of my cellmates. Going back to the cell meant that I hadn't cooperated with the guard. I shared with them the questions that were asked of me and what I had told the guard. I could sense a feeling of gratitude that I had stood firm. Yet the nightmares continued, and I resumed worrying and wondering what was to become of me and my children. How long would they keep us here? How long until they found a weak link in our little group of prisoners? What would happen if someone told? A couple days later, I found out. They came for another woman traveling with her two children. After one hour, the guard came back alone for the children. Anguished screams and cries erupted from the cell as we realized that she had sold us all out. My hopelessness was as deep as a bottomless pit as I tried to sleep that night.

Early the next morning, two of the tallest guards I had ever seen came into the cell. One held a list and told us to move to one side when he called our names. I heard the first names on his list: "Ozitaugh, Farheart ..." My heart beat wildly as I realized that this was the end of our journey to freedom. More names; it was all a blur. I saw shock, paralyzing fear, and grief written on each face as they heard their name read. All that we had risked and fought so hard for was ended as simply as writing a name on a piece of paper. One by one, the guard read the names on his list, and one by one my fellow captives let out cries of anguish and sighs of defeat.

After the guard read the last name on the list, I found myself standing alone with my boys. Immediately, my cellmates questioned the guard. "Where is her name? Why isn't her name on your list?"

The guard looked over his list one last time and silenced them with a reprimand as he growled, "Her name is not on the list, so be quiet and let's get going." He barked for the people to gather their things and get in line. They would be put on a plane and sent back. I was shocked to see that the woman who betrayed us and her two children were then brought to the front of the line and were led away with the rest of the group.

Instead of feeling hope or excitement, all the horrors of being molested and raped came flooding back. What would happen to me and to my boys? Did they intend to victimize me again? As the last person from the list left the cell, I sat back on the bed with my boys and we huddled together in fear ... all alone.

After a few hours of waiting in fear, I heard the cell door being unlocked and opened. A police officer called for us to come out. I trembled as I stepped outside of the cell. I noticed a young woman and a man. The red cross they wore on their armbands stood out against the stark white of their shirts like a beacon, and I breathed a sign of relief. They told me that they were there to take us to a place where we could stay and be taken care of until they located a permanent residence for us. Their welcome smiles warmed my cold heart, and I began to have hope. My fears of being victimized again began to fade. I remember feeling relieved that they sent a woman.

We were driven to a very nice, upscale apartment building, where we were given a huge room and separate beds for all of us! They fed us and then took us out and bought us what we needed, since all I had for myself and my three boys was contained in one small suitcase.

27

We were in Norway; we were safe. He could no longer get us. The relief flooded by body for the first time in months. I was free, and my boys were free to take a shower, to walk outside, to talk to someone, to have a friend. It seemed too good to be true. I could breathe for the first time. I remember in the jail, everyone had a secret and the fear of being betrayed kept us from forming friendships. I worried constantly they would find us, that they would take my boys from me. There was a shower, but it was nearly impossible for the four of us to get clean in it. There were people there, but they couldn't be let into my real life.

Now I could breathe and begin to live again. But the deposit that was made in my soul could not be shaken. I had been raped and I was pregnant and battling sickness that should bring joy to a mother's heart. How would I manage this new level of challenge? I had no desire to be near a man; the fear had done its evil work. As I began to settle into our new life in Norway, my heart told me we were not home; Sweden was calling to me. My friend was there—a real friend, someone who knew the real Sarah, who cared for my sons. Someone I could trust. Sweden was where I would find rest. But how, God?

I was in a safe place. I showered and dressed my children in the new clothes they had bought for us. I even had money, all given to me by the refugee organization. One side of me was very happy—my children have beds, and no one can be taken from me. We could have friends here, not to share my heart with, but someone to talk to.

About a week went by with warm showers, our own beds, freedom to walk, people to talk to, and money for the necessities. I was very thankful to the Norway Refugee Service, but I couldn't let them know why we couldn't stay—why all the wonderful things they had done for us were not enough to melt the fear from my twenty-four-year-old heart. We couldn't stay here. I needed to get to Sweden. As I dialed the number to tell my friend Sanaz where we were staying, my head told me, *you are safe, the phone is safe, the call cannot be traced,* but I couldn't trust that. My heart pounded, and the fear flooded my every word to her.

She told me that the contract with the smuggler to get us to Sweden was on hold and she would call me back in a few days and who knows what will happen then? *Wait ... wait ... Oh God, I am pregnant ... what will I tell her?* The shame cast a shadow over the hope that was trying to grow inside of me. I felt shame, I felt unclean. I had a secret ... I had been raped. It's crazy ... I was a victim. Why did this shame feel like it was covering me? And when I got there, when she saw me, when I told her, would she believe me? What would she think of me?

Now I know the truth. Every woman who is raped and molested is then attacked by the spirit of shame and fear. That spirit's goal is to continue to attack and steal and lie to her. As long as he is free to do it, in many ways the second attack is much more damaging than the physical attack. It changes your whole life and your relationships with people. But now I know there is hope, you can be set free.

I waited for a word from Sanaz, so I would know what step to take next. In our daily routine, I would remember the time when the boys and I had our meal in the restaurant on the first floor of our apartment building. They served breakfast, lunch, and dinner for all the refugees living in our building each day. There I saw some families around us with men who seemed to love their wives and children. They took care of each other and had peace. They had each other. As a child, I was a romantic girl. I had made plans to marry for love. As I saw these families, a longing started to grow in me. I wasn't envious, but I wondered what was wrong with me. Why did romance pass me by ... a girl's dream, a husband who would invite me to lay my head on his strong shoulder, who would be strong for our sons, who would inspire me to trust him, not fear him.

And now I sat here with my three children, by myself with a lot of pain in my soul and so many bad memories in my life. As I thought about the situation, more sadness and anger came over me. I turned my face from those families and tried to have a nice time with my little family, to focus on my children, not focus on me and what I was missing.

Finally, the day arrived when I called my friend, and she had news for me. "Tomorrow, a man is coming," she said. "Come out in the afternoon to the main street with the boys and get into the car that will take you to the train." *It's time to flee again,* I thought. The fear raged again. I couldn't explain this to the agency that had helped us. I didn't take anything with me—no children's clothes, no suitcase; I just walked into the street. *Act normal, Sarah; don't let anyone know.* Inside of me, I was so afraid.

I spotted the car. I said, "Hello," and got in. The man drove us to the train station, and we boarded the train. It was night when we crossed the border, another chance to be caught. The man played the part of my husband. As I settled into the small bunk with the boys he said, "The ticket collector is coming." We huddled together on the bunk bed, as he pretended that we were sleeping. All passengers were required to be awake at the ticket time. If he asked me something, I couldn't speak Norwegian. This is why we faked being asleep. The man spoke to the ticket agent in a language I didn't know, and we held our breath as the ticket was accepted and the door closed behind him.

Later, I asked our helper what had happened. He explained to me that he told the ticket agent, "That's my wife and children … they are so tired. If you want me to, I will wake them." The ticket agent said, "No, let them sleep." One more time I thanked God for another miracle.

Early in the morning, we arrived at the Stockholm train station in Sweden. The train stopped, and we got off, including the man. I was very afraid, and then I saw my friend Sanaz waiting for me. You cannot imagine how happy we were to have finished that long trip. Now we had arrived.

I was so happy to see Sanaz, I had tears of joy and was flooded with relief. We went to her house and had our first meal of one of my favorite Persian foods. I was amazed at the difficult situations God had brought us through to this point.

My friend told me her husband was worried about the money spent to hire the smuggler to bring us here, because the process had taken so long and the loan was now due. They had loaned the money from the bank, believing I would be there immediately to begin working to repay the bank. But I had taken so long, so many months, and I could feel the stress and worry that my situation brought to the house.

They said it was very difficult to get residency in Sweden. She knew many people who had been waiting up to nine years just to get an answer concerning their green card and had not yet received any answer. My joy seeped away. If they rejected my residency after all this, they could send me back to Iran. I had so much against me. How could I wait years, just for an answer that might very well be "No"? Without that card, I couldn't start working, and without work, I couldn't return the money. I had no choice, but I couldn't think that far ahead. I just had to take the next step.

The next step was to go to immigration. My friend explained that this morning, we would go down there and find out what was needed, but I didn't know what to expect. Was this the place they would bring my journey to an end and send us back to Iran? My friend explained our situation to the immigration people, concerning our flight from Iran. I was then taken to a place where a Persian translator began to ask me questions. The police asked me simple questions: "So, do you have any money? Do you have a place to stay?"

I said, "No, I could no longer impose on my dear friend. They had done so much."

The interviewer said we would be put in a hotel and given meals. As we waited for our interview, I breathed a sigh of relief; they didn't send me back yet. My friend took me to our hotel. It looked so beautiful!

The next morning, the pain hit my body in my stomach. I was bleeding so badly that I fell on the floor. My children ran out into the hall to call for help, and someone called for an ambulance. The only thing I remember is being put on a stretcher. I was unconscious. When I opened my eyes, I was in a hospital room. I was told that I nearly died from loss of blood. I had lost the baby.

Two days later, I was back at our hotel, waiting for the next bomb to drop or a miracle to happen. After a month, a letter arrived; our interview was in one week.

On the interview day, they took about twenty of us refugees from different countries from the hotel. When I looked into their faces, I gave in to worry and fear. I couldn't speak their languages. We all had secrets in our lives—some things we could tell, others we couldn't.

They took us in a police van to the immigration building, where we would be interviewed. We all sat in chairs in the waiting room. My heart was beating loudly as one by one the officers called our names. This time I had given my real name.

They called my name. I stood up and went with the officer into the room. My body started shaking. I was thinking, *What if they don't believe me? How much longer will I have to wait? I can't wait one more minute!*

My interviewer was a man of about fifty-five years old. I sat directly across from him. A translator sat to my side, but I was made to look directly into the eyes of my interviewer. Now I was even more nervous.

I said hello in Persian. My translator was immediate in repeating my reply. The interviewer snapped on a tape recorder and began to question me: Name? Children? When did you arrive?

I answered all the questions. The he started asking specific questions about my case. He asked me, "Are you here due to a political problem?"

I answered, "No. I am here because I fled with my children from my husband." He asked why. I started to share about my life, my real life. And as I did, I saw that tears had filled my interviewer's eyes. He looked deeply touched as he apologized for having to ask painful questions. I said, "No, sir. Thank you for understanding, but I know it's your job and you must continue."

During the interview, I shared my life, but didn't tell him I had been in Norway, because my friend had talked to a lawyer and found out that you must apply for refugee residency in the first country you arrive in. This was international law. But sometimes in specific situations, the law doesn't fit into your life's rules.

After an hour, I couldn't hold back my emotions anymore, and the tears fell down my face as I told him my story. I saw him turn off the tape recorder. My friend said to expect to repeat your story again and again as they try to catch you in a lie. But my interviewer never asked me to repeat a word; he just turned off the tape recorder.

He looked at me with tears in his eyes and said, "In twenty-five years of interviewing people, this is the only time I have felt in my heart I know this person is telling the truth. I don't need to question you anymore." He added, "You are still young and have your future ahead of you. When you get an answer for residency, do you want your children on your passport or separate?" He then paused and said, "No, maybe a separate passport for you, so you may travel."

I stood and asked him when I might know an answer. He said, "Lots of applications are ahead of yours," and showed me with his hand just how big the stack was.

I looked into his eyes and said, "You cannot imagine how hard my waiting is." Then I said goodbye and left the room.

After the interview, I was told to wait in the waiting room while the rest of the group finished their interviews. I sat in the room alone, and after a few minutes, the translator and the same interviewing police officer who had spoken to me earlier came up to me and offered me to take the bus home without the group. He said it would take hours to finish interviewing everyone. He then said my children were probably waiting for me. He personally took me to the bus station and paid for my ticket with his own money. He instructed the bus driver to take me to my hotel and explained where it was. I said goodbye and thanked him again. I never saw him again.

At the hotel, the worry, pain, and fear came. The next day, a letter came saying I must prepare to leave; my interview was over and now we would be moved to another city, to another refugee place to wait for the answer about the residency. Two days later, they came to move us. The new city was four hours from Stockholm and from my friend's house.

Another new place, more new faces. I met many people in this place, waiting for our residency—some from Iran, some from other countries. They had been waiting years for their residency answer, four, five, seven years. When I heard this, I remembered the policeman's reply: "There are many applications ahead of you." In a way, I was happy my children were safe, but I could not wait four years without an answer. I had to repay my friend. My situation looked better; we were safe, but there was no peace inside of me.

There was a translator available to us and an assistant to help the refugees with questions. One day, the assistant, Andish, asked if my children would like to take swimming lessons at the refugee center. It was summer. I said, "Yes! Yes! May I learn too?" They said yes. It was so much fun with my children in the water. Many other refugees were there too.

A month later, the assistant called me to his office. I missed my friend Sanaz, so he gave us permission to take the bus to Stockholm. It was very good to see her, but I really felt the strained situation in the home because of the loan.

I prayed all night and slept in the next morning. Early the next morning, the phone rang and Sanaz answered it and then handed it to me. I sleepily said, "Hello?"

It was my assistant translator from the refugee center. He said, "Sarah, you must come back as soon as possible."

I felt my heart drop as I cried, "Why? What happened?" I was really scared, wondering why he would call me at my friend's house. Why was he asking me to come back now? And then he said the words, "Congratulations, Sarah, you have received your residency!"

My eyes popped open as I let this miracle settle on me. "What!" I screamed.

He said, "I know. We cannot believe it. We've never heard anything like this before. We don't understand it ourselves, but you had better get back here. Maybe it's a mistake, because it is not possible after just one month."

A long scream of celebration started out of my mouth. "Oh God! Oh God! You did it! You did it!" I think the walls were shaking at this moment as I remember an escape that had been building in my soul from the beginning of my journey across that bridge. We jumped up and down and screamed and laughed and cried for the first time in forever.

I hurried from my friend's house and drove back to the city I had been visiting from. I met with the assistant, Andish, and inquired about this amazing news. "Is it true?" How can I have received my residency after only one month?"

Andish replied, "I know, it doesn't make any sense. This has never happened before."

I was taken to the refugee office and showed my documents to the official. "Yes, this is all in order. There is no mistake. Welcome to Sweden!"

Immense joy erupted again as I screamed *thank you* again and again. Those who did not know my story looked at me with an amused smile and nodded awkwardly at my antics.

Andish took me back to the hotel, and I rushed to share my miracle with those with whom I had been living and waiting with. But I then saw the bewilderment and anger in several people as I was celebrating my residency. I immediately realized my celebration was causing others pain. Many of the immigrants had been waiting four to seven years and still had not even heard if they were going to be granted residency papers or not. My heart went out to these people, for I knew the pain of the journey and of waiting so long for a dream to come true. I decided I would keep my celebration private, so as not to rub salt in the wounds of other less fortunate people.

Life was looking up. I was so happy with the residency papers, I could hardly contain my joy. After two or three days, the translator summed me to come and speak with Andish again. I went to Andish's office, and he told me that he had received a letter from the police. Andish looked confused as he relayed through the translator, "Something very unusual has happened. I am sure there must be a mistake this time! This is crazy. Your passport has arrived."

Andish took me to the police station to inquire about this news. Once there, Andish handed the letter to the police officer, who returned with an envelope. He handed me the envelope, and I removed the small booklet. It felt unbelievable to hold my own real passport in my hands. This meant that I could begin working, get my own apartment, and really begin to live. But then another miracle happened. I did not only receive my passport, but three other booklets fell from the pages of my passport—one for each of my boys, Cyrus, Kevin, and Alex!

Our passports did not have our pictures, so we went back to get the boys. We returned, and in a matter of a few minutes, our pictures were taken, and right there in the station, they were stamped onto the passports and were handed back to me.

The system was set up so that once a refugee received their residency and passport, they were then moved to apartments in other cities—usually less-populated places where it wouldn't be difficult to find an apartment. The officials made the decision of where to send refugees. Most refugees waited several years before they actually moved into an apartment of their own. Another miracle happened when I asked the officials if it would be possible for my family to be sent to Stockholm to wait for an apartment. My friend lived there, and I wanted to be near people I knew. To my amazement, they agreed to my request, and we were sent to a government-subsidized apartment in Stockholm. There we had two rooms and much nicer conditions, and my children and I were enrolled in school to learn the language and to be acclimated to our new culture.

Everything was new: new people, new surroundings, and things were so much better. I was so thankful to God for rescuing me from destruction. I was appreciative to all the people He used to bring me to this place of freedom. It was a new chapter in our lives, with many blessings. Yet I need to tell you it wasn't the end of the pain in my heart, the sore in my soul, or the nightmarish memories in my mind.

I tried my best, but even on my good days, I battled feelings of depression, shame, anger, and disappointment for what I had been through. I held on to unforgiveness and hatred toward the perpetrator of my abuse. I also mourned the loss of my mom and my family in Iran. I enjoyed the companionship of my friend, but she also had a family and a job and couldn't be with me all the time.

I began talking to a counselor about my experiences, hoping that I could get some relief from the pain I was carrying around. But all the counselor could do was listen as I retold my story. All the pain surfaced again. My bleeding and wounded soul was exposed, in hopes of finding healing. But all the counselor could offer me was some sleeping pills or anti-depression medicine.

Just changing locations or situations doesn't change the grief, the burden, and the shame that attaches itself to a heart. Yes, I was physically free, but my heart was still deeply wounded and still very much in captivity.

I longed for peace and rest. I wanted to live in a quiet area and get away from all the noise of the apartment hallways where we could hear noisy people at all hours and children crying. There were too many people to ever have peace and quiet. I was very tired. I knew that it could take up to two years for them to locate a permanent apartment for us. Our names were very far down on the list.

I talked one day to the assistant of the government housing department and asked about the possibility of getting a place of our own sooner. She listened to my story and told me she would see what she could do. After a few days, she called me to her office and told me that she would consider our case a special situation and move us up on the list. She showed us an old three-bedroom apartment. It was dirty and very much in need of paint.

It wasn't what I would have chosen, but I was so ready to be in our own place that I told her I would take it.

I didn't want to bring my children to this new home, with it being so run-down and dirty. I decided that I would go every day and paint as much as I could while the boys were in the care of the refugee center. I purchased the paint and began to transform our new home. One day, I was finishing up on my painting and was very tired. My fatigue turned to fear as I received the news that Alex, my four-year-old, had been hurt and was at the hospital. I raced to the hospital and was told that he had been playing with some other kids and had gotten knocked down and broken his arm. The women who brought him to the hospital told me that Alex never cried once. He was very concerned for me. He kept telling the ladies, "Don't cry! My mom will feel bad!" He was so afraid that he would make me sad that he paid no attention to the pain of his broken arm.

When I got there, he looked up at me with his bright blue eyes and said, "Don't feel bad, Mom. Nothing is wrong. I'm okay!" My heart broke as I realized my little boy at the tender age of four was that concerned for me. It gave me the encouragement to be strong and to live for my children.

I brought Alex home to our refugee apartment. The painting of the walls was finished at our new place, and I moved our family to our private apartment. Now we had passports, residency, and a home. They even gave us a government loan just for necessities for the apartment. I only bought a few things for my dear boys, secondhand things for myself, and secondhand furniture.

Our daily life began. Cyrus and Kevin started elementary school, and Alex went to preschool. Our apartment was very close to the preschool and school, which was such a big help. The boys could walk across the street. Cyrus and Kevin started learning Swedish with a tutor at school. Each morning, I would wake and make breakfast for the boys before they went to school. I was learning Swedish too, three hours every morning, because I needed a job. The government supplement money was only for food, but not enough to pay back the loan.

I started looking for a job. My friend's son taught me my first Swedish sentence: "Do you have a job for me?" I also had it written on a small piece of paper, which I kept in my pocket in case I forgot how to say it.

My first job was in a cafeteria. They asked me what time I could start. I was hired to bus tables, take the trays when people finished eating, and fill water glasses. All I could say was *"Ya."*

In my culture, as an Iranian woman who had been a beautician instructor, I sometimes felt humiliated to be cleaning up after people finished their meals. But I needed the money. The loan to pay the smugglers was still unpaid.

I remember one day it was my turn to clean the restrooms. I locked the door and began to cry, "Oh God. This job feels so bad. My loan is due soon. What will I do?"

When I came out, the restaurant manager asked, "Sarah, what did you do in Iran?" I told him I had been a hairdresser. He said, "If it was up to me, I would keep you here always. You are good with people, very gentle, but why don't you try to be a hairdresser?"

Then I started thinking, maybe I could, even without knowing the language. I could learn in Swedish very quickly the exact questions to ask the clients what needed to be done to their hair.

The next day, I walked in to the first salon I saw and said my sentence, "Do you have a job for me?" In broken Swedish, I explained that I was a hairdresser.

He said, "Can you start tomorrow?" Wow, another miracle! I went back to the cafeteria and told the manager that I had taken his advice and had gotten a job in a salon. He was happy for me.

The next day, I started my job. I was asked if I had ever cut men's hair. I hadn't. In Iran, I had only cut ladies' hair. I had to learn to cut with a man's clippers. I asked him if I could watch him for two days while he cut. I did. I was ready to work now, but he didn't want to ruin his customers' hair. So I brought in my friend's son and showed him what I could do. He was really surprised. He couldn't believe that I could do it after only two days. So I began to work as a hairdresser again.

I have one funny memory. After about one month, a man came in. He looked like a professor with a suit and tie, very nice and proper, with a beard, which is very rare in Sweden. I asked him, "Can I give you a cut? How would you like it?"

He said, "Just a little thin on the ends."

So I began. I took out the clippers and started. It looked good. I got to the sideburns, and I trimmed one. He had a beard, and I had cut him a sideburn. His beard now had a separation on the left side! Oops! What was I thinking? He said, "No, please!" I was so shocked that I had done this. I was getting used to the standard cuts and totally forgot about his proper-professor beard. I asked him if he wanted me to do the other side too. "Oh, no!" The miracle was he was kind to me and said not to worry. He even came back again!

The months rolled on. My friend asked me how I was communicating with my clients. I replied, "I don't. When they talk to me, I just nod my head and say, *'ya, ya.'*" Oh my, what must they have thought? What was I agreeing to? Heaven knows!

I was paying on the loan to my friend's husband every month. I had been working one year and decided to get my own loan to start my own salon. I bought my first little salon. It was a very good place, but the seller didn't have many customers, so I got to purchase it at a very low price. I was happy. I started painting my own salon. I put down a nice floor, put up pictures, ran advertisements. I even went out on the street and passed out flyers to the many office workers who frequented the area.

Our financial situation started to improve. We were surviving, paying our loans, and even helping others. I was a busy woman and a busy mom, all without a car. I remember carrying the plastic bags of groceries home through the snow in the winter, falling, and crying. I loved my boys dearly, but they were still too young to help me. One of the common meals for me was homemade frozen pizza. We could just pop them in the microwave.

Life continued: I was busy making it, but still the pain remained inside me. The mask that had hid my pain had just been replaced by a new one. I was free, things looked good on the outside, but the bad memories were still with me. I had fled from my bad situations in Iran, but I couldn't flee from myself. I continued to talk to a psychologist, but whenever I spoke with her, I just remembered more.

At night as I watched my boys sleep, I wondered if they missed their father. I knew they missed having a dad, but I couldn't be that for them. Kevin loved playing soccer. I would look at that beautiful face, and I knew that he missed having a dad cheering for him. But I had to work, take care of many things. It was so rare that I got to be there for him. I felt very bad, but I couldn't do anything about it.

Cyrus was starting to grow up. No matter how much love I gave him, he needed a father as a role model. As I would look into his eyes and knew many things he was feeling but there was nothing I could say, nothing I could do but continue working, continue pouring out my love on him, and do my best for his future.

My baby Alex was young, full of energy, and beautiful, but he didn't remember very much about his father. But still the need was there; the hole was there.

I would sit at night with these things on my heart, but I didn't mention them to anyone. People were busy with their own challenges, their own lives. I tried to put these thoughts out of my head and sleep.

Every day had a pattern: breakfast, school for the kids, and work for me, even if I was sick or overwhelmed. I had to make money for a debt I had to pay and three boys to support. I tried to do my very best for my family. I tried not to think about our past, yet it was still there.

A family member told me my husband Ali had sent people to Sweden to kidnap the boys. The nightmares started again, except this time the boys were in school and I was at work. I sat and talked with them over and over about never going with anyone. I was passing my fear on to them. It was very difficult, and I didn't know what to do. They were so young and innocent, so easy to be deceived by someone who was being hired to take them.

I told them about their dad's plan. I told them never to go with anyone and never to open the door to anyone, not even the police. When I looked into those eyes, I saw the pain and fear on their faces.

There was a playground in front of our apartment. All their friends played there, but I couldn't let them out. This lasted a year. Fear and even aggression and anger arose because of the situation we were in. I was young and in trouble. I needed someone to take care of me, but I had a job, and if I wasn't working, I had to get home and guard my precious boys. Their freedom was gone again, and even the psychologist couldn't help make things right during this time.

As the next year started, we were still together. I had spoken with the schools and the social workers. Everyone assured me all was being done that was possible.

I decided to ease up on some of the rules. The boys needed some freedom. I said they could begin to go out some, but even Cyrus, my oldest, must return no later than 8:00 PM.

Word reached me that my husband had remarried and had a new child. I felt a little relief. I felt the hope that he might let us live our lives. I finished paying off my debt, and the boys were making friends. I began to have friendships too. We even took a vacation.

One summer I sent the boys to a camp in Sweden for two weeks. They had a lot of fun with other children and their camp leader. I got to have a vacation as well, touring and resting. Having fun with my friends was a new experience for me, to say the least. Finally, we had money for what we needed, even things we just wanted. There were no more worries about how we were going to manage or about what we had to do without. So much of our lives had involved skimping and doing without. My outside situation had completely changed, but my inside situation had become infected. It was beginning to turn to gangrene in me. Now, whatever I wanted I could have.

I thought back to Iran, when Ali was beating me and holding me prisoner. All I had was that one finger—hidden but free. I'd put that finger under my sweater and whisper to myself, "You are free, little finger." Now my whole body was free. I could do whatever I wanted. My children were with me, and no one was going to take them. I could go wherever I wanted to go. I would talk with myself and ask, "What is wrong with you, Sarah? Why do you feel this way?" At that time, I didn't realize my body was free but my soul and thoughts were still in bondage.

As a Muslim woman, I prayed to God, but every day I felt that inside me, nothing was changing. Actually, it was getting worse every day. Also, as a young woman, men were trying to come into my life and propose marriage. I couldn't have any of that, because I didn't believe in marriage any longer. To me, marriage was a curse. Also, I thought even if I did want to marry, I couldn't imagine letting someone discipline my children, no matter how good a husband he was or how much he loved them. They had been through too much. It was an impossible thought. That's why I thought of marriage as a curse. I hid all my dreams of having a "happily ever after." It was amazing to me that as much as I was hurt by men and as angry as I was at them, through it all I still had the dream that I did as a young girl, for my Prince Charming, my "great romance."

I felt the big hole in my heart by this unmet desire every day. One day I was dressed up and I put my usual "mask" on that I wore in front of others. I was invited to someone's birthday party. I was sitting in my beautiful dress in a pretty home, watching people chatting. A fourteen-year-old girl named Pega was looking at me for a long time. I knew a lot about her life. Her parents were divorced; she lived with her stepmom and brother. She wasn't treated with love by that stepmom. After a few hours of her looking at me, I asked her, "Why are you looking at me so much? Do I remind you of someone? What is it?"

She said, "Sarah, you are so pretty; your clothes, your car is great. When I see you, I think your life is perfect with no problems, and I wish I were you."

I looked at that fourteen-year-old face and did something I had never done before. I reached over and whispered in her ear. I told her, "Honey, you don't know what you are saying. You can't imagine what I went through. What you see right now is just part of the mask."

She, with her beautiful big brown eyes, gasped. Pega couldn't believe what I had just shared with her. I couldn't believe what I had just said, the truth about me. But from the outside, people saw a strong woman with a strong personality and pride. I never would share with anyone the inside of me, the romantic heart, the pain, and the weakness. I would wear the make-up, the fashion, and have the strong attitude. Every day, I didn't even look in people's eyes, but I was really bleeding on the inside. My mask covered all that. The opposite was the real truth. No matter what amazing story was told, I hardly ever smiled and I never laughed. I had too much pain inside of me. It was just ridiculous to me. Nothing was fun to me, and people mistook this mask for pride. Little did they know under it all was the bleeding, wounded heart of a deeply romantic girl who was screaming, "Help me!"

My salon did very well, and business was very good, so I bought my second salon. I had my beautiful car and my beautiful home, but every day when I went to work, depression would settle in. I couldn't sleep at night, so I took pills to sleep and pills for depression. I felt no joy. It felt like the end to me.

One day, my day began as usual with the kids going off to school. I went to work an hour earlier than I usually did. I was there by eight. I felt more depressed and tired than usual. I didn't feel I even had the energy to drive my car, so I took the tram. As I sat there, I surveyed my past year; 1995 was coming to a close. I began making notes about the state of my life. I should be writing how I now have everything I want. I have my freedom, I have my children with me; I am successful at work. I bought my own home. I have a boyfriend. I have everything I need. Why am I writing about how empty I feel? Why do I feel imprisoned when there is no jailor? Where is the joy? I didn't feel I had the energy to pursue the elusive "it" any longer. I sat there puzzled by myself, with no one to explain it to me. *Maybe next year will be better* was my only conclusion.

The new year came; 1996 didn't come in with a bang—just a dull changing of the calendar. Day after day passed—force myself to go to work, come home from work, feed the children, bedtime, and toss and turn as I faced the night. Every night the memories were waiting for me as I lay down to try to sleep. Everything that I had run so far from was waiting for me as I lay my head down. The images were inside of me, and I couldn't get away from them. There was no way to run from my own thoughts. After an hour or two of wrestling past them, I would find a troubled rest.

One night in particular, things were different. After wrestling past the memories, I fell into a deep sleep. In the middle of the night, my deep sleep was interrupted. Suddenly, I heard a very powerful man's voice calling my name. "Sarah," I heard. I sat up in my bed, ready to respond. I heard his voice two more times calling my name. I felt a presence. There was instantly the awareness that someone mighty was in my room. I opened my arms as if to receive a hug. There in my room, I was caught unaware, unaware of the joy that could be mine in the presence of a mighty God. Yes, I was filled with pain, every sore in my heart aching; all the while I was conscious of the fact that I was a sinner, but the mighty God had come to me. He was in my room and He hugged me. I didn't know such a thing was possible, but every cell in my body registered his touch. I felt overwhelmed with joy. I felt love. There is no way to explain the feeling I had in that moment. It goes beyond the best time I ever had. It goes beyond any love ever experienced with a man. Better than the satisfaction of any material object, sweeter than any sunrise or sunset. Truly there is nothing to compare it to in the natural realm. These were my feelings, but I also felt His joy, as if this moment had been long-awaited. He was as happy as I was. And then He was gone. I laid my head down and slept like a baby who had just been held by her father. The next day, I recorded my date with God.

This experience was amazing for me. Ever since I was a child, I perceived God as someone who could do whatever He wanted. So if He decided to hug me, He could hug me. So as I said, it was amazing but it was not a concept that was entirely new. As a child, I would ask my mother, "Mom, can God see me?"

"Yes," she would reply.

"Can He see me all the time?" I would ask.

"Yes, all the time; He is a mighty God," my mom would explain.

As a Muslim girl, I would pray three times a day. Before prayer, I must wash my hands, arms, and face; I must also cover my head and my body. If I had nail polish on, I must remove it. When praying, I must also speak the prescribed prayers in Arabic. These were the rules. In order to pray, this is what I must do, my mom taught me. I remember asking my mom why it is that God needs me to cover myself when I pray, when he sees me without covering other times, and also why I must talk to him in Arabic language that I don't understand and say the same words every day. She would quickly retort that such questions were sins and to quit talking like that! "Go and do your prayers." So the questions remained inside of me, but I dared not ask such sinful things again.

The effects of this experience filled me with energy. I would go to work and feel good. My life felt good. Physically and mentally, I felt great for about four days. Little by little, the effects wore off, and soon I was back to the old familiar feelings. After a while, I hardly remembered that God had hugged me.

Darkness returned. The memories were back. From childhood, I had a fear of the dark, and it was back. The nightmares were back. The suffering of missing my mom was back. At this time, I felt like I was at the end. Thoughts of suicide were rising up in me again. Suicide had occurred to me before when I felt that I was at the end. In those times, the only reason I pushed those thoughts away was to live was for my mom and my children, only because I knew what it would do to them. I knew that my children needed me, not only for their circumstances and situation in life; they also needed my love and support. These thoughts were not enough to stop my line of thinking anymore. I continued to think of suicide, no matter what it would do to my children or my mom. For a few days, I considered how I would do it. I told no one. The mask stayed intact. I was an expert with the mask.

On Saturday, I went to work as usual for my four-hour shift from about 11:00 AM to 2:00 PM, my weekend hours. My hands went to work on my clients, but my mind was busy thinking about how this would be the last time I would do this. When I finished with the final client, I walked the usual five minutes to my car. As I was walking, my thoughts were busy figuring out how I would do it. Would I take pills, would I cut my wrists?

I looked up to find myself in front of a large building with wooden doors. It was as if I had just woken up from my thoughts and found myself in front of this building. I entered the building and I saw a cross. It was a church. I entered it, looked around, and saw that no one was there. I didn't understand why this building was unlocked. This is not the usual habit in Sweden. I knew about Jesus somewhat; even as a Muslim, I had some knowledge of what Christianity was or Buddhism or Hinduism. I began to talk to Jesus. I said to him, "Jesus, I have prayed so much to God and to the people that I have had faith in, but no one has answered me to give me peace. I know that in the Christian faith, they say you are the Son of God and you died and you resurrected again, but in my faith as a Muslim, I believe you are a prophet, and I want to share about my life with you."

So I began to tell Jesus about my life from childhood to the present time. I don't know how long it took. But at the end I said, "If you are really the Son of God and you died and resurrected again, then you should be able to hear what I am saying to you. I am tired of myself and everything in my life, and I cannot handle it anymore. That's why I'm about to kill myself.

45

If you really hear me, can you do something in my life? Because I give up, I cannot go on anymore." After I said this, I looked around, and nothing happened, no one was there. I thought to myself, *Are you crazy, Sarah? You are talking to the walls.* I was very angry.

Then I stood up and took my purse from the floor. Suddenly, my eyes connected with a painting on the ceiling of Jesus being taken down from the cross. My eyes connected with His eyes. They were real. Not like "real eyes" that you sometimes see in a painting that seem real. They *were* real. His eyeballs were moving and blinking like a live person.

I was fixed on His eyes. He looked in my eyes so deeply. He looked inside me. His eyes were filled with love and compassion and pain. He didn't talk with audible words, but I felt the words inside of me so strongly, it was as if I could read his eyes and they said, "It is not my will that you suffer like this."

When I saw this, I started shaking and crying. After a few seconds, I looked at the painting to see that His eyes were now closed. I stood up, took my purse, and walked to my car. I cried all the way to my car—openly. People along the way could see me; I was embarrassed, but I could no longer wear the mask. I made it to my car and drove home. I came home to my children, but I did not mention any of this, not to them or anyone.

The next day was Sunday, and I received a phone call from a friend. She was talking to me about church and Jesus. We had never discussed either of these subjects before. During this conversation, she invited me to church that morning. She said it was Pentecost Sunday and the church was celebrating this special day. I said to her, "I don't want to hear anything about God or church or Jesus. I don't even know what Pentecost is." I hung up the phone. A few minutes later, someone else called me. I barely knew this person; my friend put her on the phone to invite me to church. I asked this person, "Why do you want me to come to church?"

She said, "The pastor in the church told me, Jesus said to call Sarah and tell her to come to church, I want to do something in her life today." When the woman told me this, I remembered how I asked Jesus to do something just the day before. I had told no one, and now I was being invited to church for the second time this morning. And furthermore, Jesus said to the pastor to tell Sarah to come to the church. When I heard this, I started crying again. I asked her for the address of the church. I hung up and got ready as quickly as I could. When I went to the church, there were many people present, two floors of people. It was a big church. By the time I got there, it was close to the end of the service. I sat on the first floor, close to the back. I sat there looking at the people around me, full of anger. It was my first time ever in a church with people. They began to worship. They played the piano and guitar, and the people clapped. I thought they were crazy to worship God this way. *Music and clapping, what are they thinking?*

I was filled with hatred as I looked at their faces. Then the pastor began to talk. He said, "Today is Pentecost. If you want to be filled with the Holy Ghost, come to the front." He said he would pray for them. I had never heard of such a thing. But some of them went forward, and as he prayed, some of them began to fall to the floor. I looked at him and said to myself, *Ha, he's doing hypnotism.* When I said that, the picture of Jesus's eyes came to me. Inside of me, I said to God, *God, there are many religions, and everyone thinks theirs is right. But, God, who has it right? Is Jesus really your son? Is Christianity really the true way to you? Are the other religions made up?*

If Jesus is really your son, and he died for sins and resurrected after three days, and if this man is really praying and the Holy Ghost is really touching people and it is not hypnotism, then touch me right now, right here. Then I will believe in Christ. When I said this inside of me, suddenly I felt a power come over me, and I felt like a puppet. My hands and arms began to wave around quickly, and I didn't have control over my body. Even my tongue, I began to scream in Swedish, "Jesus, I love you! Jesus, I love you!"

After a few minutes, I fell flat to the floor. At that moment, God through his Holy Spirit, in the name of Jesus, delivered me from darkness. As I sat up, the people gathered around me and said, "It's a miracle, it's a miracle!" The feeling I had when I entered the church, the feeling I had when I watched the people's faces, was changed. I didn't hate them anymore. I felt so light, as if I was a bird that could fly. The feeling was so amazing, so beautiful. It was peace like I had never had before. The pastor then asked for people to come forward to receive Jesus in their heart. I went. I gave my life to Jesus. I asked God to forgive my sins. I invited Jesus into my heart and my life as my Savior, as my Lord, and as my God. I came back that same night and was baptized in water and the Holy Spirit.

I sang all the way home. I screamed out the windows that I am saved.

That night, as I lay in my bed thinking of all that had just happened, my mind went back to a childhood thought. When I was a little girl, I would think about how one day I would stand before God. I knew that He would decide heaven or hell for me at the end of my life. I had a secret plan inside of me for that day. I thought that God would only be aware of things that I said. In other words, if I had a thought that I had not voiced, such as my secret plan for facing God in the end, then I could trick him. My plan went like this: as I stand before God and He is deciding to send me to heaven or hell, if it is hell, I will ask Him for only one wish. That will be that I could look into His eyes. I figured that when He would look into my eyes, I would captivate Him with one look and He would fall in love with me and be unable to send me to hell. As I thought about my childhood plan, it occurred to me that Jesus had turned the tables. He used my own plan on me. As I stood at the brink of hell, He showed me His eyes and captivated me. I fell in love with Him and was unable to take my own life. Wow! He read my childhood secrets and drew me into love for Him. What a personal God. He's the Almighty God, and yet He used my childhood secret to present himself to me. I was amazed at His humility to show Himself to me like this. For the first time, I slept without medication. I was done with the pills that put me to sleep.

The next morning, I awoke with such joy in my heart! For the first time, I woke without the feelings of weariness and stress in my soul. I felt like I could fly! Something strange, new, powerful, and beautiful had happened to me. I no longer needed to hide behind a mask. I was a butterfly emerging from her cocoon—totally and completely me, the way God created me.

I never had read the Bible before and had no concept of the term "born again," but I now know that this was an authentic "born-again" experience. As a Muslim, I had learned about religion, but I had never expected this complete and total renewal of freedom and joy and peace. This experience of a personal relationship with God! It was as if the Lord had poured out a waterfall of love over me and totally washed away all the pain, shame, and scars of my past.

One year before I accepted Jesus, I had met and began dating a man from my town. We would meet for lunch or dinner or go to the park. Over time, I developed a bond with him that I thought was love. I was never taught about God's plan for holiness in dating, so our times together would, at times, include showing physical affection.

After I was saved, I recall a time when my boyfriend placed his hands on my shoulders to give me a hug. My body began to shake and tremble, and I remember the distinct feeling of something leaving my body. I was confused about this. I tried to begin to read the Bible, but I would open it up and begin in the middle of stories, and to be honest, I was confused. It seemed every time I opened it, I would read about Jesus multiplying the loaves and the fish. It didn't have any real relevance to me at that time.

One day, I was at my salon, and a woman whom I barely knew came in and told me, "Sarah, the Lord has put you on my heart to pray. So I am praying for your salvation."

I laughed as I joyfully told her, "Oh, I have already accepted the Lord!"

"Oh, well then, do you read the Bible?"

I told her I had been trying but always seemed to read the same part about the loaves and the fish, and I just didn't get it. She laughed and said, "Oh, you need to begin at the beginning of the gospels. Start in Matthew and read all the way through." We talked, and I told her about the strange experience I had recently with my boyfriend. I told her how I had trembled and had since felt a little less joyful, like there was something wrong—not so much between my boyfriend and me but between the Lord and me.

The woman asked me about my relationship with my boyfriend. I told her he was just my boyfriend. I never wanted to get married. My experience with marriage was tainted. I grew up believing marriage was the same as bondage and was nothing more than a curse. She told me that God created marriage, and if I want to live my life holy before God, I could not have a relationship with a man outside of marriage. This was the first time I had ever been told this. She left, and I had some time alone with God.

"God, I want to understand your Word. I need you to help me to understand and apply what you tell me in the Bible. Will you please help me?" After that, I opened my Bible and began reading in Matthew. True to His word, He did open my eyes, and the Bible became real and relevant and personal to me! Tears of joy and revelation flooded my eyes as I read. Several times I needed to go to the restroom to dry my tears before my next client. I am sure my customers thought I was crazy, but I didn't care. The Word had become life to me, and I was devouring it like a starved woman.

I got to the story of Jesus fasting for forty days. I recalled the conversation with the woman at my shop. I wanted to live a life pleasing to God, and I desired holiness in my life. At that moment, I felt led to begin a forty-day fast and to seek God's will for my relationship with my boyfriend. I said to Him, "Lord, you alone know the plans you have for me. I want to know if this man is the one you would have for my husband. If he is, then I will marry him, but if he isn't the one you desire for me, then please take away the feelings I have for him, Lord."

I fasted breakfast and lunch, but I didn't stop there. I told my boyfriend that I didn't want to see him or talk to him for forty days while I sought the Lord about our relationship. Of course, he thought I was nuts and he was angry. He called and tried to see me several times, but I wouldn't answer the phone. It was hard. I wanted to talk to him; I did miss him terribly, but I would just ask the Lord to give me strength to hang on.

One day, near the end of my fast, my boyfriend showed up at my salon. I remember feeling drawn to him. He looked very cute, and I really had missed him. I found myself wanting to go to him and give him a hug. Yet I wanted to remain faithful to the whole forty-day fast. I wanted to be obedient to what the Lord had asked me to do. I silently pleaded with the Lord, "Jesus, help me!" I felt very weak.

At that moment, I saw a bright white light from the corner of my eye. It was almost blinding in its brilliance. I sensed that it radiated directly from my face out toward my boyfriend, who was seated next to me. All at once, without me saying a word, my boyfriend shrank back in shock and what looked like fear and said, "What's wrong with you?" He immediately got up and left the shop. I never saw or heard from him again.

I found out several months later that my old boyfriend was not who I had thought he was. God had saved me from marrying the wrong man and had kept me safe from more emotional harm.

I became involved with a small group of Iranian Christians. We met in people's homes. It was nice worshipping the Lord in my native language with other believers who came out of Islam. It was great sharing our testimonies together. I bought myself a very large white marble cross necklace and began to wear it. My clients noticed. They asked me, "What's happened to you, Sarah?" They asked me if I was still Muslim. I told them I had received Jesus in my life. It was my salon, and I could do what I wanted, so I told them the whole story of what Jesus had done for me. No more pills for depression or sleeping, no more psychologists. I felt completely new.

One night, I was home with my boys, Cyrus, Kevin, and Alex. They were very happy to have a new and improved mom. I was no longer tired, angry, and sad after work. They had a mother who just enjoyed being with them. They didn't understand everything, and sometimes I'd see them just looking at me strangely. I had just gotten home from work and made dinner. Shortly after that, the phone rang.

"Hello?"

"Hey, Sarah, how are you doing?"

"I'm good."

"Well, listen, at work there is this guy from Iraq. He's a super-religious Muslim—almost dangerous. I never speak about Jesus to him, but he asked me about my haircut, and I recommended you. So, just be careful and don't talk about Jesus to him."

I answered, "Can't promise anything. I have to do what God tells me. He can come tomorrow at 2:00 PM. See you later," I said.

I let him know the time. That morning, I prayed. I ate with my kids, sent them to school, and headed out for work. Around 2:00 PM a man in a suit with a crippled left hand arrived for a haircut. It was the Muslim from Iraq. He sat down and I put the cape on him. As he looked at me with my huge white cross necklace, he started questioning me. "So, are you Iranian?" he asked.

"Yes."

"You are Muslim. Why do you wear that cross?"

"I was, yes, but I received Jesus in my life, and now I am Christian."

I saw his ears begin to turn red as he shouted, "God has no son!" I explained to him that I believe God is one and is expressed also through Jesus and the Holy Ghost.

He really lost his cool then and stood up from the chair, yanked off the cape, and screamed, "How can you do this? It is wrong! You are Muslim." I saw such hate and anger in his face. I really believe he would have punched me if we had been out on the street. As he was storming out of my salon, I felt Jesus say to me, "Sarah, tell him I'll meet him very soon."

And before he yanked open the glass doors, I called out to him, "Excuse me, sir, Jesus says to tell you He'll meet you very soon—but not the Jesus you know. I mean the Lord Jesus, Son of God."

"Ahhhhh!" was all I heard as he slammed the glass door with all his might.

Days passed, and each day was a new joyful adventure sharing Jesus, doing my job, and taking care of my children. About a month after I met the Iraqi man, he showed up again unannounced at noon at the salon. He was carrying a bundle in his arms covered in tissue paper. "Do you want a haircut?" I asked him.

"No, I just came to deliver this to you. Someone sent it to you."

I was a bit scared now. "Who sent this?" I asked.

He said, "Jesus." Now I was really scared. What was he up to? I noticed he did look different. With newfound peace in my heart, I opened the tissue to find one stem of white baby's breath flowers … just that. It's usually added to a bouquet, but it was given to me alone. It meant something to me—to God and me from a long time ago. Something this man could never have known. This is something that could only be Jesus. The tears immediately started flowing down my face. That man's presence was definitely changed. I didn't see any more anger and hatred. As I asked what he meant by all this, he said, "Last night, when I was in my room, Jesus came to me. He told me He would give me three wishes, three desires. I told Him what they were and He said, 'It is done.' Then He came over to me and put his hand on my heart, and as he did, I could see inside of me. My heart was now shining out through the flesh. It looked like crystal. Then Jesus handed me this flower for you and said, 'Give my regards to Sarah.'"

Right then, I remembered what the Bible says about God taking away the heart of stone and giving us a heart of flesh. I asked him, "What do you say about Jesus now?"

And with all the sincerity and passion that was held in his new shining heart, he shouted at the top of his lungs, "He is the true God. Jesus is the true God. He is the true God!"

And I joined him jumping and screaming, "He is the true God! Jesus is the true God!"

Never before in my wildest princess dreams had I ever imagined being so loved and so desired as I did that day in my salon, holding my special flower from my prince, Jesus.

My nights were filled with talking with Jesus, and my days were filled with seeing His blessing and presence in my life. Everything was amazing to me. My children and I were looking for a new home, because the area where we were living was beginning to change. New apartments were everywhere, and new people were moving from different areas. I wanted my boys to have roots and culture to be part of—a nice house with a garden. Our new home was in a nice Swedish community. We had all new things: new furniture, a beautiful two-story home, a real blessing. The boys were excited, but Cyrus was seventeen and didn't want to leave his friends, so I asked the Lord to change his heart and let him be happy there.

I remember going out and buying them waterbeds they really wanted. We bought three new waterbeds, and even one for me. So we moved the beds into the beautiful new house filled with beautiful things and a beautiful view and even a flower garden in the yard.

One day, my friend Hannah called me in the salon and said, "Sarah, I'm tired from working. Let's go out for a nice dinner this Friday."

I said I would like that and hoped Cyrus would watch the boys for me. I was looking forward to my dinner out; it had been a long work week in the salon, and I really needed a nice night out with my friend, Hannah. Around 3:00 PM, I got a call from Mary, an older woman who hosted our believers group in her home each week. "Sarah," she said, "I want to invite you to come tonight and join us in our prayer meeting."

Many times I had been in her home, but never had I been asked to come to the Friday night prayer meeting. I told her that I would be able to tell her later and thanked her for inviting me. I was really torn. Part of me was ready to go out to dinner and relax and be with my friend, but the other part of me just couldn't pass up the opportunity to go to this prayer meeting. I called Hannah and told her the situation, how I wanted to be at the prayer meeting tonight and wondered if we could go to dinner another time or maybe she could get other friends to go. She listened to me and I felt very bad. "If you want me to still go with you, I will," I told her.

She said, "No, Sarah, it's okay. Go to that prayer meeting."

I went home after work, got the boys dinner, and spent some time with them. Then I got ready to go to my first prayer meeting. Maria's house was about forty-five minutes away, so I had time to talk with the Lord. "Lord, you said in your Word that whenever two or three are gathered in your Name, you are there in the midst of them. Is it really true? Will you actually be there with us at this meeting? Or will it just be a bunch of people talking and praying? Jesus, I just canceled my plans with my friend. Is this really true? Are you really coming as your Word says?"

I drove the rest of the way to the meeting wondering about that question. How can the Lord be in the midst of us? I arrived at Maria's two-story villa and was welcomed into the group. There was Maria and her husband, four other couples, and a five-year-old son of one of the couples. We shared dinner together and had a time of worship. Their living room furniture had been arranged in a large circle, and we all found a seat, as a man began to share a message about the gospel. As we were listening, the young boy got up and went and whispered something to the man speaking to us. We thought it strange and wondered what he had said, but the man simply listened, and then the little boy went back to playing on the floor nearby.

The man finished his message and instructed us to close our eyes and begin to pray. The room was quiet and serene, as one by one we offered our petitions to the Lord. Suddenly and without warning, we heard loud footsteps descending from the wooden stairs of the villa. Boom, boom, boom! The footsteps were powerful, strong, and certain. They were footsteps that came from one in authority. We were all startled, because there was no one else in the house. We stopped praying and looked toward the steps in fear, wondering who was coming.

The man then spoke up. "Close your eyes and continue to pray. The boy told me that the Lord had spoken to him and asked him to tell me that when we begin to pray, we will hear His footsteps among us. He said 'Don't be afraid, because it is the Lord.'"

Everyone else immediately went back to praying, but I couldn't believe my ears! How could that man have known the conversation that I had with the Lord on my way to this meeting? I was overcome with awe of the Lord and fell on my face before Him, weeping and rejoicing and praying. "Oh Lord Jesus, you are amazing! You are beautiful! You are true to your Word!"

After that experience, anytime I heard of a prayer meeting, I tried to be the first one there! I would even ask to be invited. I knew in the deepest places of my heart, as His Word says, "When two or more are together in my name, I am there in the midst of them."

I was filled with such joy and peace and love. I was simply amazed at the changes that were coming over me. Before, I was filled with rage and hatred, but now I had a peace that surpassed my understanding. Hurtful words and hurtful people no longer had power over me. I found myself talking about my Jesus everywhere I went and to anyone who would listen. It made no difference to me what they thought or how they accepted my words. I shared about Jesus with as much joy and pride and excitement as my heart could express.

Jesus became my idol. I no longer looked to people. Christians and non-Christians alike have a sin nature and make mistakes. Even pastors fail sometimes. People will disappoint us and let us down. But when we keep our eyes fixed on Jesus and His Word, then we will not be disappointed. I've learned that no one is perfect except the Lord. One day we will be made perfect, but for now He is working on us, perfecting us little by little until the day when we see Him face to face.

My life had dramatically changed, yet I want to tell you that in my children's lives, nothing had changed. They were young men now and still harbored all the pain, bondage, and rage from the events of their childhood. Yet, because of my relationship with the Lord Jesus, I could deal with my boys and relate to them and love them with the love of Christ. I rarely talked to my boys about Jesus. I simply lived a life that showed my love and adoration for the Lord. I loved them with the love I had been shown. This was such a help in parenting them.

There are so many children who are raised in the church from infancy. They are in the church all the time, yet many only know about religion and have totally missed out on a personal relationship with Jesus. My children were never brought up in the church. They never attended a Sunday school class or youth group. But God used my life as a living testimony to them. I simply allowed my life and my love for Jesus to be seen. And when tough times came, I would simply remind them that Jesus loved them and that Jesus was their Father.

My mother was living in Iran. She had become very sick, coughing all the time. One day on the phone, I spoke with her and realized how sick she was. I was very sad. I couldn't leave Sweden to be with her under the circumstances. The "old Sarah" would have been depressed and completely devastated. The new Sarah, Jesus Sarah, had that peace that is not found in the world. I couldn't imagine how I would have gone through this without the Holy Spirit in me.

I still hadn't told my very religious Muslim mother that I received Jesus in my life. She had truly kept all the laws. I loved her very much. In some Muslims' minds, Christians were unclean people without God in their lives. This would have tormented my dear mother, who really spent her whole life as a dedicated Muslim. I didn't want to break her heart. It had been many years since I had been able to spend time with her. She wouldn't understand this about me.

One day, I was in my house with the praise music on, and I was worshipping the Lord. Suddenly, I felt the Holy Spirit speak to me, saying, "Sarah, call your mom right now. Talk to her about Jesus." I didn't know what to do but ask for strength. I received it when I immediately felt the presence of the Holy Ghost with me in that room. I dialed the phone.

"Hi, Mom, it's Sarah."

"Hi, Sarah, what are you doing?"

"Mom, I have to tell you something so important. A very amazing and wonderful thing has happened to me."

Now, at this point, I am sure my mother was waiting for me to announce my engagement. You see, it was her prayer that someday I would marry a good man. I could feel her excitement, which only added to my anticipation.

"Mom, I'm not Muslim any longer. I received Jesus in my heart."

There was a dead silence. All I could hear were crickets chirping.

"Mom, Jesus isn't just a prophet. He is God's Son. Mom, He came to this earth to forgive our sins. Those who believe in Him as the Son of God will be forgiven of their sins."

More silence. A fire began to burn in my bones. My mother spoke. "What do you mean? What are you talking about, Sarah?"

I began to explain. "Mom, think about this. God, He is like the ocean. If you take a glass and fill it with ocean water, it's just a small part of the ocean in a cup. Now, Mom, if you take a test strip and put that into the ocean water and put another test strip into the cup of ocean water, it tests to be the exact same water. He is the same taste, Mom. If you drink from the cup of ocean water, it tastes the same as if you put your mouth on the ocean and drink from it. That's why Mary got pregnant through the Holy Spirit. Jesus didn't have an earthly father. Jesus was the Son of God Himself. That's why He's one with God. The same Spirit that got Mary pregnant is the Spirit that came from God. So, Mom, that's why that cup and ocean I told you about is the picture of Father, Son, and Holy Ghost. You see, Jesus is the cup and God is the ocean. The Holy Spirit is the water in the cup and in the ocean. Mom, that's why they are three different forms but one spirit, and we also believe in one God."

Now I breathed. Now I was quiet. What would be her response to what I had just told her? I was pacing my house with the cordless phone, just speaking the words that came flowing out of my mouth. There was so much passion and conviction. I kept thinking to myself, *What would she think of me?*

The next words I heard were the sweetest words I could ever have imagined.

"Sarah, what should I do now to receive Jesus?"

I was shocked. I couldn't believe what my ears were hearing. My mother was the only one I was scared to talk to about Jesus. I was just dreading to tell her I had received Him, and now here she was asking me how she could receive Him too.

I know my mom tried to live her whole life for God. She had really tried to live a holy life. Now I knew the truth. It doesn't matter how holy you live your life or how sinful you live it; each one of us needs forgiveness from God through Jesus Christ.

"Mom, that prayer I prayed, could you please repeat every word after me? That is the prayer of salvation."

"Dear God, please forgive my sins. I confess them to you. I am a sinner. I believe you sent Jesus, your Son, to die for my sins. I believe He rose from the dead after three days. Now, Jesus, I invite you into my heart as my Savior and Lord. Amen."

"Hallelujah!"

She repeated every word. I told her how much I loved her and how much Jesus loves her. Also, I told her now He is not only your God; He is your Heavenly Father, too.

After I hung up the phone, I had to pinch myself. I didn't know if this conversation was real. It was too good to be true. Tears began to flow down my face, but they were not tears of sadness, they were tears of joy. I worshipped the Lord again. I was very thankful for the Holy Spirit's prompting and very happy I obeyed. I learned that day that what looked impossible to the world is possible to God if we would be sensitive to the Holy Spirit's voice and trust him.

A short time later, I had invited Mom to visit me in Sweden for a month. When she came off the plane, she looked so much older. It had been many years since I had seen her. She stayed with me for about a month. We prayed over her and spent time with her. We really enjoyed each other's company. She saw how God had blessed me: the beautiful house, a car, and the passion I had for my sons. I really had joy, and she could see it.

At this time, our home group church was growing up. We had an Iranian pastor and his wife. He would share the gospel with our group of Iranian believers as we came together at Maria's house each Sunday. One day, our pastor announced that he and his wife would be moving to another city and he could no longer be our pastor. We continued for another month at Maria's house without a pastor. Maria even asked me to step into that calling. I was a new believer. I was an evangelist with no calling to be a pastor. I told her, "No, thank you." Every one of us has some calling on our lives in the body of Christ. It's very important we stay in what God has called us to do.

One member of our home group, Neda, suggested a Swedish pastor who was willing to come to our Sunday gathering and preach to us in Swedish. Since many members only spoke Persian, Neda said she could translate it for the group as he preached.

He started coming each Sunday and preaching the gospel, with Neda translating. After about three months, suddenly our old Iranian pastor and his wife returned. He took control of the group again, and no one questioned this at all. The Swedish pastor was dismissed.

Neda came by the shop one day in tears about the situation. She believed this was wrong and started talking about the possibility of starting a new group in a new location. She was very emotional, and I really got caught up in the moment. My emotions took over. I didn't really ask the Lord about what she was saying. I was a new believer, and I really wanted to do something for the Lord! Neda said rent would be our main problem, and I said not to worry about the rent because I would pay for it. I told her to go and find a location. I also asked her not to tell anyone that I would be paying the rent. I really wanted to stay anonymous. It was something between the Lord and me that I felt I could do for Him.

Neda found a place and signed the lease. We started meeting. I provided cookies with coffee and tea after each meeting. I made sure no one knew I did that either.

I talked to many people about Jesus, as I felt led by the Lord. Neda told people as well. We invited them to join our Sunday group. When people told me they couldn't get there because they had no car, I offered to pick them up and take them home. I drove many people from many different areas.

Sundays became an all-day event, with all that driving in my beautiful Audi car. I called myself a "taxi driver for Jesus."

Our first meeting was attended by a few people. But then it began to grow and grow. Many people did fall in love with Jesus, but others fell in love with "Sarah's services," as I was also trying to meet their weekly needs of a ride to the store, shopping, or whatever else they asked.

During this year, our little group grew as we met each Sunday. We even began to collect a little offering. Also, at this time, my original home group at Maria's house lost their Iranian pastor for a second time. Many began to join with us. This was very exciting. Neda had just finished a two-year Bible school.

One day she announced that she felt we should start charging for the cookies and coffee. I reminded her that it was my secret gift, and she ignored me. Each Sunday, we would minister to the Iranian people who came. I felt the presence of the Lord so much with me as I completely poured out God's love for those people and felt their love back for me. At this time, Neda's attitude toward me began to change. She was a single mom like me, but I saw an agenda beginning to rise up in the things she did. She displayed pride about herself and jealousy toward me, along with the love I shared with those dear new believers. Many of them were refugees like I as one time. I saw myself in their faces, they had difficulties with their economy because of the situation they where in. I began to wonder about Neda's "plan."

Each week, she became colder to me. She embarrassed me publicly in our meetings every chance she got. I really wanted to do what Jesus would do, so I loved her and took her abuse without a word. The old Sarah would have fought back and hated her.

Then she told me it's been a year and half now that we have the old home group with us. She said she would be the pastor and we didn't need the Swedish pastor any longer. Suddenly an alarm began to sound in my heart. I told her, "Neda, if God really called you to be a pastor, that is very important and wonderful, but you just finished Bible school. Being a pastor takes more than head knowledge. Don't you think you should take steps slowly as God gives you the heart experiences to share with them?" She didn't look like she liked that idea.

After that conversation, things got worse for me. I overheard her saying mean things regarding me. Members of our group came to me and tried to tell me these things too. I had to say to them, "If you tell me something, let me go and speak to Neda face to face about it. If you can't allow me to do that, please don't tell me."

But each week I could see the truth in those stories.

One day, I felt so bad, I wanted to straighten out whatever it was that had changed her attitude toward me, so I called her and asked to meet at her place. When I arrived with flowers, I hugged her and poured out my heart about wanting reconciliation. I asked her what I had done to cause her to dislike me. I told her, "The new believers are being confused by your bad treatment and words about me. You aren't just hurting me. If it was just about me, I would take it as a sacrifice, but you are hurting Jesus really bad."

We talked for a while, and she assured me with many words that she was sorry and things would change. But the next Sunday, nothing changed, except she was even worse to me.

My thoughts at this time were about our people, not who should be pastor. I had no problem with Neda being pastor if she really believed she was called, but it was her attitude and her heart that showed me otherwise. I know no one is perfect; not I, not Neda, and not even the pastor. However, if you are the pastor, people are going to look at you very closely. They are looking to see the heart of Jesus in what you do. Neda's heart wasn't there yet. If she continued in this way, the people would just begin to leave.

Two Sundays later, we arrived to find that Neda had dismissed the Swedish pastor and put herself in his place. She began preaching every Sunday. As I listened to her, I could see that she feared she would lose the people if she didn't give them what they wanted to hear. So each week she tickled their ears and stayed away from the true gospel, believing this would keep the people coming.

After a while, people began not to show up. Even our old home group left to go with a new Iranian pastor. Our big group dwindled to thirteen or fourteen people. The very thing she feared was happening. The true gospel may cause some people to be convicted and leave for a while, but God is at work in their lives and they often return changed. People will never change if they don't hear the true gospel.

I felt very bad during this time and didn't know what I should do. I wanted to leave—maybe even go with the Iranian preacher or even attend a Swedish church, but I didn't want to leave the dear few who were still there.

After a while, I left the church. I couldn't continue there; I had no peace any longer. I started attending a Swedish church, yet still helped out my other old Iranian church on Saturdays. Neda continued for about six years. A few would come through, seven or eight, and they always left after a few weeks.

Neda's pastoring was short-lived. She went back to translating for another Iranian group. She then left that group to return to her own private life.

From this hard experience, I learned a good lesson: try to never do anything out of emotion or because of a situation … especially if it's for the Lord. Always ask Him first. Pray. Wait. Be sure it's His voice and not our flesh.

I believe the reason I never left the Lord or His church was because I had a real relationship with the Holy Spirit. Jesus promised to send Him to us after He left the earth to explain things to our hearts. I would often sit and pray and quietly wait and listen for the Holy Spirit's instruction and encouragement about the things that were happening in my life. He would help me with what to confess, what to take action on, what to forgive, and where I must change. When Jesus was on earth, He spoke to the people. Now the Holy Spirit speaks to those who want to wait and really listen to Him. It is very sad; some people have forgotten to listen and obey the Holy Spirit.

I was a new believer, and this whole "church problem" was a big disappointment to me. It really could have caused me to stay away from being part of His body through the church. But I chose to obey the Holy Spirit. Thank God for His mercy and grace as He looked down and saw my heart and the real motivation behind what I did. Out of my mistakes, He brought blessings to many people and to me as well. Sometimes people make their own decisions in their private lives or even what they want to do for the Lord. From the beginning of whatever it is, we forget to ask God if this is okay with Him for us to do. Then, when things fall apart, we blame God. We ask Him, "Why did you let this happen?" We forget to ask for directions on what to do from this point on. We forget to ask forgiveness for our part in the mess. Then bitterness begins to take root deep within. As a result, many people leave the church at this point. If they stay, they leave behind the relationship with the Holy Spirit and try to survive on religion alone. I thanked God for this valuable lesson. I became even more sensitive to the Holy Spirit.

One day, at the church, I saw a woman about my age. I felt the Holy Spirit urge me to go to her and give her my phone number. As I did this, I told her I didn't know why, but asked her to call if she ever needed anything.

One day, a year later I received a phone call: "Hello, Sarah, it's Farrah."

"Who?" I asked.

"You gave me your number last year at the church."

"Oh, yes. Yes, I remember you. What can I do for you?"

"Sarah, I'm out on the street with my suitcase. The police are going to deport me to Iran. Can you help me?"

I went to the place where she was, picked her up, and brought her to my home. She lived with us for a year and a half. I treated this young Muslim woman as my own child. I told her about Jesus, and after a year, she received Jesus in her heart and was baptized.

I hired a lawyer and helped her with her paperwork. She received her residency in Sweden during the next six months. This was a true miracle after six years of waiting.

She is now married and has her own home. I thanked God for the privilege of serving Him this way.

During the time that Farrah lived with me, I received the most heartbreaking phone call of my life. My brother called from Iran. "Sarah, I have bad news. Mother has died."

My heart skipped a beat as I screamed, "No! It's not true! Where is she? Put her ear up to the phone and I will pray for her, and Jesus will bring her to life!"

My brother, a religious Muslim, stammered, "Sarah, what is wrong with you? I have buried Mother. She is dead, Sarah! You are talking like you are crazy!"

My head was spinning in dread and confusion. My thoughts flashed back to the death of my father when I was a girl of nine. This was such huge loss in my life. Like a stab to my heart, I remember watching other children with their fathers and feeling this intense pain again. I struggled for years with the grief of losing my father. After my father died, my mother became my world. She was mother and father, and I loved her. I could not—no, I would not accept this news from my brother! I hung up and felt like my mind was in a fog. How could this be true? I had dreams of one day going back to my country and seeing my mother again. I could almost see her face as she opened the door. I could almost see her eyes twinkle with delight and joy as she and I embraced.

I went through the next few days going in and out of denial about my mother's death. It was like a nightmare, except this one was true.

After about three days, the Lord reminded me of how He became my Heavenly Father when I accepted Jesus as my Savior. I remember how He took away all those years of grief over losing my father. The Lord actually became my Heavenly *and* my earthly Father! I was completely delivered from the grief. He became as real to me as any earthly father could be and He still is!

I went to my room and knelt before the Lord. I began to talk to Jesus. "Lord, you alone know how much I loved my mother. You know how difficult this is for me. Oh Jesus, this burden is too heavy for me to bear. You said in your Word that if we have any burdens, we should come to you. Well, I am coming to you, Lord; I cannot go years in grief for my mother like I did for my father. I am asking you to take this burden now, Lord. I am giving it to you."

I wept in surrender and suddenly felt the sensation of something being lifted out of my body and taken out through the top of my head. All at once, I felt this unspeakable joy begin to well up in me. True to His Word, Jesus had taken my burden and replaced it with His peace! I had a memorial ceremony in honor of my mother in Sweden. Friends could not believe the freedom and the peace that I had! They were crying for me, and I saw in their faces their confusion. *Why isn't she crying and screaming in grief?* I know they thought I had lost my mind. They all knew how dearly I had loved my mother and expected me to be grieving deeply. We had three pastors at her memorial service, and one of the pastors shared these words: "Some of you may wonder how Sarah can be standing here with a smile on her face and not weeping with grief. Well, it's because of Jesus Christ, who takes our grief and our burdens upon himself and gives us

His peace. Jesus can do this for you too. Invite Him into your heart, and He is faithful to help you."

The pastor prayed, and two Muslim friends accepted Christ at my mother's service!

I want to tell you, our Lord is faithful and He knows when we are serious in our surrender. Sometimes we can say the words but our actions don't match up. We can say we are surrendering a problem to Him but we continue to worry. This is not total surrender. For example, what if you had a bill that you could not pay and you asked a trusted, faithful friend to help you by paying the bill for you? You would need to give the bill to him and trust that he was going to pay it! You wouldn't keep going back and asking to see the bill and taking it back again and again. You would trust that your friend will do what he says he will do. We need to trust Jesus with the requests of our hearts. The Lord sees our authentic hearts and He honors our sincere requests.

In 1999, a pastor from Miami, Florida, came to our Swedish church to do a Bible study for one month. He was a wonderful man with a wife and three grown children. I liked him immediately; he was so full of passion and humbleness. I invited him and a group from the church to come over to my house for dinner. As I was serving them, he looked at me and said, "Hello, Cinderella." I remembered the secret from my childhood memory. In my heart, I was Cinderella. I was so happy and excited this man of God, who knew nothing about my childhood secret, said this to me.

In early 2000, the pastor from Miami invited some of us from our church to come to Miami for a conference. I really wanted to go, so I took my two-week vacation time from work. Instead of going to the beach, I went to the Miami Bible Conference with my friend.

For the conference, my friend and I stayed at that pastor's house. Every day we went to the church for the conference. I was able to share my testimony and minister to people. Everyone was very nice, inviting us to dinner and shopping. Many people gave me their business cards and phone numbers, inviting me to keep in touch with them. It was great to be around so many believers, worshipping together.

Before I left for the Miami conference, I was over saying goodbye to my neighbors. They are a Muslim family from Iran and very good friends.

They knew I was Christian now. As I was leaving their home, the husband asked me, "Hey, Sarah, when you are in Miami, can you buy me a nice bottle of tequila? I will pay you back for it."

I told him, "Sure, no problem." I wanted to show my love and not make him think it was about money. As I was walking out the door, I was already wondering how I was going to ask someone from my Christian conference to take me to the liquor store.

My friend and I enjoyed the conference together. She had brought her son with her and decided to extend their stay two weeks longer to spend some time on the beaches. They left me three days before I headed home to Sweden.

The next day, after they left, I still had not purchased my neighbor's tequila. I had to do this. I didn't want him to think it was about the money. I really didn't want to ask the pastor; I was embarrassed. *I'm here for a wonderful Christian conference and he doesn't know me that well. What would he think about that request?* I made my decision to ask him. I went to his home office, knocked on his door, and asked to speak with him.

He probably thought I wanted to confess something as he invited me into his office. He said, "Yes, Sarah, how can I help you?"

I told him in my broken, limited English. "Excuse me, Brother Raul, I need the tequila!"

I could see his eyes behind his glasses pop as he asked me, "What, my dear?"

I struggled in my limited English to explain to him how my Muslim neighbor had asked me to buy him a bottle of tequila. I saw him breathe again as he said, "Okay, Sarah, no problem."

He sent me out with his nice fifty-five-year-old assistant named Anita. Her job that day would be to take me anywhere I needed to go. I explained to Anita about what I needed. She took me to a large liquor store that also sold other things. As we entered the store, a gentleman in a tie and short sleeves opened the door for us. He followed us and asked us what we needed. Anita said, "Tequila."

He took us to that aisle and began talking right to me, describing the brands. The he started showing his interest in me as we listened. He told me, "You are so beautiful. Can I have your number?" I said no. He said, "At least can I have a hug?"

As I was standing in front of all that tequila, I had no idea what to do. I started explaining my broken English and that the tequila wasn't for me, it was for my neighbor in Sweden. Anita came to my rescue, asking him "Do you work here?"

He said, "No, I just like her," as he pointed to me. "I just followed her into the store."

Anita said, "Get out of here!" And he still begged for one hug before he left.

I said, "No way!"

He left and then returned in a few minutes with a present in his hands, saying, "Please, if you won't give me a hug, at least accept this present from me."

I think he thought I'd hug him after I took his gift, but I did not. Anita said, "Okay, she took your present, now go!"

We quickly bought our tequila and went to our car and opened the bagged present. He had presented me with fire-engine red lipstick! We laughed our heads off. I told Anita about a movie I had seen on TV once about a crazy killer who would seduce women. Anyone who went with him, he would kill them and then write on their bodies in red lipstick. So I told Anita maybe he was that crazy killer type. Maybe because I didn't go with him, he gave me the lipstick that he intended to use on my dead body.

Anita said, "Sarah, I don't think he's that type." She also said that never in her life had she had such an experience.

When I got back from Florida, the Lord started talking to me. I remembered something before I received Jesus. For many years I would go to fortune tellers and many types of mystics. I was desperate to have a word about my future. I would go to these places often. Now that I was a Christian, I read in the Bible that the Lord hates sorcery, witchcraft, and fortune telling. This is not the Lord speaking. He didn't want me to go to these places any longer. I made a firm decision not to, even though the desire was still there.

The Lord showed me that some people begin to do "right things" because of the fear of the Lord, but they still suffer with the desire. It is because there is a spirit behind that desire that needs to be delivered out of them. I was fearful at first about this, but the Lord said, "Don't worry, Sarah, I am with you and I will deliver you from this."

I heard there was going to be a conference in Holland. It was a Iranian conference but there were also believers from all over the world. More than a thousand believers would be there. There would be many different preachers and Derek Prince was one of them. The service would last from morning to evening. Derek spoke about deliverance during two of those days.

I sat as close to the front as I could. I was in the second row as he spoke about deliverance, bondage, and the spirits behind it all. A thousand people and forty pastors listened to him speak.

He said, "I know many people are listening. Some people will believe what I say and some won't, but I have a lot of experience in this matter. Even with believers when I've prayed for them, they have been delivered from different spirits."

Then he said, "Please close your eyes and ask the Holy Spirit where the Lord wants to deliver you." As he said these words, I remembered that the Lord had spoken to me before this conference and showed me what it is I must be delivered from. I already knew. Oh, how I loved Jesus at that moment. He had led me here for this deliverance.

Derek Prince asked us to put our hand over our head as he called out spirits that Jesus would deliver us from. The first one he called out was the spirit of divination, witchcraft, and fortune telling. He spoke out to this spirit, "In the name of Jesus, leave these people." Then he continued calling out the other spirits like lying, lust, religion, pornography, etc. I heard many people crying out and falling on the floor. I felt something strange happen in my body, and something left me. It was amazing after that, I never ever had the desire to go to fortune tellers again.

I also heard testimonies from many Christians there about the many deliverances and healings that happened that day. We thanked our Heavenly Father for His great work through the faithful Name of Jesus, His Holy Spirit and His servant. The conference ended, and I returned to Sweden happy and *free!*

When we attend a Christian conference, we have such a great opportunity to hear from the Lord. Go with an open heart and focus on God. Listen for Him to speak to you. There are many true believers in one place, so expect the Lord to bless you, deliver you, and show you new things. Don't take a Christian conference for granted. Expect God Himself to move on your behalf.

I continued my journey of faith with the Lord. One day, I decided to visit my friend Karen at her hair salon. We spoke briefly, and she got busy with a client. Just then, I sensed the Lord asking me to go and ask the young woman working nearby if I could pray for her. I felt awkward and shy and wondered if I had heard right. I began to argue with the Lord. "Lord, do you really want me to pray for this girl? I know that she is a very religious Muslim. How will she receive me? I really don't want to do this, Lord." I busied myself with other things in the shop while my friend was working on her customer.

The Lord persisted in His request. "Go, Sarah, ask her if you can pray for her." Finally I surrendered and timidly went to the girl and asked her name.

"My name is Pari," she told me.

I shared with her that I had converted to Christianity and felt that Jesus wanted me to pray for her. Her face registered a look of shock and surprise, and then she burst into tears as she told me her story. "My mom was in an accident, and she has been paralyzed. The doctors said there is nothing more they can do. They said there is no hope. My mom is young, and they say she will be paralyzed for the rest of her life."

I said, "Well, I will lay hands on you and I will pray for your mom." I called my friend, who was also a believer, and we went to a private area in the back of the shop to pray. I prayed, "Dear Heavenly Father, you are the God who heals us. You said with man, it is impossible, but with God, all things are possible. Please touch this woman's mom with your healing hands and restore her body in Jesus's name."

I left soon after, feeling relieved that I had obeyed the Lord to pray. Several days later, Pari called me to thank me for praying for her mom. She was healed! I told her I was happy about her mom but that Jesus, not I, was the One she should thank. I told her I was happy that she told me, because now I would also thank my Heavenly Father.

A few months later, I was visiting another friend, a new believer, at her house when the phone rang. I overheard her consoling someone on the other line. "Oh, I'm so sorry; wait! You know Sarah, the one who prayed for your mom? She is here now! Do you want to talk with her?" The answer must have been yes, as she handed the receiver to me. It was a very upset and tearful Pari! I was shocked that this friend even knew Pari, and I was amazed that she should call during the time that I was visiting her friend! Just goes to show that our God is able to set up divine appointments as He wishes. I asked about her mom and found out that her mom was fine but the problem she was having now was personal.

"Sarah, my husband and I have been married for five years, and we have been trying to have a child. I just found out that I am unable to conceive. The doctors said I will never be able to have a baby. I love my husband and he loves me, but I am so afraid that this news will break up our marriage. We have wanted a baby so badly. I am just devastated!"

I reminded her of what Jesus did for her mom. "Pari, the same Jesus who healed your mom is able to heal you. I am going to pray for you in Jesus's name."

I prayed, "Heavenly Father, nothing is impossible for you. I come to you and ask that you open Pari's womb and make her fertile so that she and her husband could conceive a child. I ask this in Jesus's name." Our God is so good! Only one month later, I received a call from Pari that she was pregnant! I thanked the Lord and told Pari, "I am bringing you a Bible so that you can read about the One who has done great things for you! You need to know Jesus personally, Pari." She happily agreed. I dropped off the Bible to her at work. My faith was growing by leaps and bounds, seeing Jesus so actively working and how He is so merciful and kind to even those who do not know Him. I was learning more and more about the power of the name of Jesus, but what He would show me next was supernatural!

I was enjoying learning from God's Word. I was like a sponge, soaking up all that I could read. I told the Lord in prayer that I would love to go to Bible college one day, so that I could learn even more about Him. I also told Him that this would be difficult, since I had my job and my children to take care of. That night, I had a dream of Jesus and me sitting side by side. I was holding the Bible, and Jesus had His arm around me and was teaching me Himself, pointing out Scripture as we sat together. I awoke the next morning with such joy in my heart. What a wonderful dream! I arrived early to the shop that morning.

Shortly after I opened the door, a stranger came in. He was a man in his fifties with white hair and a white beard. His eyes were very unusual, hard to describe except to say that they were "special." He had a bouquet of white flowers wrapped in tissue paper and a small box, also wrapped beautifully. He said, "Hi, this is for you."

I was shocked, and before I could say anything, he asked my name. As I told him my name, he slowly pulled out a small, plain white card and wrote these words on it: "May God bless you, Sarah, with joy, hope, and love." He then handed the flowers, the gift, and the card to me, said not a word, and left the store.

I was so curious and taken by surprise, I immediately opened the gift to find a new Bible. There was an olive leaf marking a page, and when I turned to it, my eyes fell on these words: "The Lord is coming back very soon." I felt that this must surely be an angel of the Lord. I ran out of the shop to look for the mysterious man, but he was nowhere to be found. I never saw him again.

I continued my day with joy, knowing that I had just experienced an encounter with God. I found out at church about a conference that was to be held in Sweden, about six hours away from our town. I had been mentoring a woman named Miriam who had just received the Lord the week before. I felt that this conference would be an encouragement to her and her children. Miriam had gone through a divorce due to her husband being involved with drugs. After about four years, she was converted from the Muslim faith and she received Jesus in her heart. She was beginning a new chapter in her life, and the Lord had placed her on my heart to be an encourager for her. I went to Miriam with the information of the conference. I did not have the time to go with her, so I suggested that

Miriam attend the conference on her own. She told me that it would be difficult for her to go with her young children on her own. I offered to go with her to support her. I didn't want her to miss this opportunity to grow in the Lord, so I arranged to take the time off, and made the decision to go with her. I made the room arrangements and signed up for the conference, which was to last one week.

The night before the conference, Miriam called me. "I'm so sorry, Sarah; I cannot go to the conference. I am in so much pain! I don't know what has happened to my back, but I can't move!"

I went over to her house and found her stiff and unable to move from her position on the couch. I sat down, and Miriam started chatting to me nonstop about various topics: her children, her back, her work. All the time she was talking, I was having an internal talk with the Lord, while smiling and nodding at the right places in Miriam's monologue.

Father, it's obvious she is in pain and cannot go to the conference like this. What should I do? Should I pray for her? What if you choose not to heal her? Then her faith may falter, and she is such a brand-new believer! Lord, she doesn't even know about healing; maybe if I pray, it would freak her out and her faith would suffer. Oh, Father, I need to know what to do!

Finally, I submitted and said, *Okay, Lord, I'm just going to do my job and pray, and you do your job and heal her.* I told her, "Miriam, I am just going to pray, and I believe the Lord is going to heal your back and you are going to the conference tomorrow!" I prayed and laid my hand on her back. "Heavenly Father, you are the God who heals us. Please touch Miriam's back and heal her so she can go to the conference tomorrow."

All of a sudden, Miriam jumped up and exclaimed, "My back doesn't hurt anymore!" God totally took away her pain and showed Himself faithful! I helped her get herself and her children packed and left for home.

We left early the next morning for the conference, which was about a six-hour drive from our town. We arrived, and the man who was in charge of assigning rooms remembered me from a former conference I had attended earlier that year in Holland. The Lord has a way of changing a person from their former sinful attitudes, and this process happens little by little over time. During the last conference, I had complained when he had given me a room assignment with a woman and her two young children. I had been so insistent that he had found me a single room, just to make me happy.

Mehde greeted me cheerfully. "I have your room assignments, Sarah; you will be with three other adult women."

"Oh, no," I said, "I want to room with this lady and her children!"

He smiled. "What has happened to you? You complained at the last conference that you didn't want to room with children! Now you do? What has happened to you?"

I answered, "Yes, Brother Mehde, the Lord changes us. We don't become perfect overnight, but if we are listening to Him, He comes to change every weakness in our life, little by little."

One morning after the conference, I was in my salon, preparing for the next day as always, when I heard the Lord speak to my heart so clearly that there was no denying it was Him and not me. He said, "Sarah, I want you to sell your shop and all you have. I want you to serve me 100 percent now. No more haircutting. I want to use you in the world starting with Bible school in the United States."

As this statement shocked me, I gasped. I couldn't escape this life-changing moment. I sat in the back room of my salon and began to cry out to my faithful God, "How, God? How can I do this? I have three sons and a house payment. Lord, these two salons. How can I?" It was then at that moment I recalled, exactly one year ago a woman from church had come into my salon and spoken these words. She said to me, "Sarah, I believe the Lord wants this for your life, to sell all your possessions and go study the Bible in the United States." I had smiled at her face, but laughed in my heart, saying to myself, *You are a crazy lady. There is no way I could ever do that. Doesn't she know I have three sons, a house payment, two salons and employees—completely crazy woman?*

But now, in front of the Lord, I cried because I couldn't deny this was His will for me, and as always, He would take care of all my needs. As I sat weeping at the hugeness of this revelation the Lord had given me, my phone rang. It was the same lady who had spoken those words over me one year ago at that exact moment—as if to seal the deal between God and me. She greeted me. "Hi, Sarah."

As I replied, "Hello, Laura," my voice was quivering.

She asked me, "What is wrong? Why are you sad?"

I couldn't talk about this thing yet, so I said, "It's okay; I just had a little cry."

She asked, "What happened?"

Just then, a customer walked into the salon. "Laura, I have a customer. I will call you back later." I hung up the phone and went to do a cut.

Afterward, I sat and thought, *Lord, I serve you. You spoke this thing to me. It's a big step.* I could no longer deny. My whole body confirmed that this was the Lord. "But how?" I asked. My children were still living with me. The year was 2000. Alex was fifteen, Kevin was seventeen, and Cyrus was twenty. How would we continue to eat and pay with no more money coming in?

Again, the phone rang in the middle of my questioning the Lord. It was Laura. She said, "Hi, Sarah." Her voice was very excited as she continued, "When I heard your voice on the phone, I asked the Lord, why is Sarah sad? I prayed for you. He answered me and told me to pick up the pen and write down each Bible verse that he would give to me."

Now, Laura was not very accomplished in Bible verse memory in any way, so this was very significant to be coming from her. It had to be the Lord. Laura said, "Sarah, this is what happened. The Lord said, 'Laura, pick up the pen and write down what I tell you.' He just started giving me chapters and verses throughout different places in the Bible. He just gave me the chapter names and verse numbers. I really had no idea what these verses were about in the Bible, and the Lord said for me not to look them up myself, but just to call you and give them to you, Sarah."

After I copied them and said goodbye to Laura, I was very excited and ran to open my Bible. I started to read back these verses in the exact order that they were given to me. They formed a personal letter to me from God out of the Bible, as perfect as if He had set the pen to paper Himself.

And so it began, out of Job. "The Lord gives and the Lord takes away. Naked you came into this world and naked you will leave it." The first thing out of His Word to me spoke to my deepest fear about money. On and on and on it went, as He spoke to me about the future life. He has planned for me. After I read my personal letter from God, a supernatural peace settled over me. I went home from my salon that day with a completely new direction, with a new focus—a mission.

Within a week, I began to speak about what God had shown me. And as I did, I was very surprised by the reaction I got from some people. At church, I was called crazy and by some, even demon-possessed. So I continued to pray and ask God if this was really Him. He gave me dreams and visions. I could not deny this plan was 100 percent God, no mater the reaction of some people.

The next hurdle for me was my precious sons. I was dependent on them. I loved them very much. They were dependent on me also. Cyrus, Kevin, and Alex were still at home with me, but I knew I could trust the Lord. I didn't even mind what people said about it.

I sold my salons and began to search for Bible colleges. One person told me about a school in Dallas, Texas, called Christ for the Nations. So I planned to go and take my youngest son Alex with me. I applied and was accepted. My visa was sent. Next was my house. It was big; it was too big for just Cyrus and Kevin. And the Lord had said to sell everything. At this time, I heard the Lord's voice again. He said, "Sarah, you have proved yourself to me. You love me more than your job, your home, and even your beloved sons. Now you need to know I love your children even more than you do. They need you. Stop the sale of your home and stay with them. The time is coming when I will send you, and I will tell you when that time comes."

I had sold my salons. Through my tears, I knew He was preparing me and I would follow Him. His love for my children and me amazed me. He knew about my love and my need to be with my children. He understood. He loved them more. Wow! I was amazed all over again. I was learning a lesson to trust Him with my most precious things of the heart. He knew me.

Now I felt I was alone, floating in the ocean. I had wanted the people at the church to be able to support this move of the Lord in my life, and now I was staying after I had told them the vision—after I had applied to Bible college and been accepted—after I had sold my two salons. This was very hard. I knew that God was teaching me to follow Him alone and not to be affected by the people's reactions. Whether they declare you crazy, demon-possessed, or whatever—follow God.

Still, I knew as a church we are called to be one as Jesus's body. We were to work with each other. But now I was seeing a new lesson, that sometimes the Lord calls someone to something specific that everyone may not understand prior to asking God about it. As a church, we should not try to shut down that person's vision with our disapproval or personal judgment. Rather, we should first go to God and ask Him to show us what is happening and pray for him to bless the thing, if it's His will to open the person's eyes or if it's not His will.

It's very important that we do not judge the person with our words but give them kindness. If we really have an interest or concern in the matter, go to God and ask Him about it. Ask Him what He says about this thing. Look at Jesus. He treated people differently according to the call on their life. He didn't tell every person to leave everything and physically follow Him. To some He said, "Go home and tell people what I've done for you."

So now, I had decided to go the Bible college in Sweden. I didn't have to work, so I wanted to learn more about the Bible while I waited for the Lord's time for United States Bible college.

During the first month of school, I came home to a letter from my gynecologist. I was given a date to come for my six-month check-up. I arrived for my Pap test and went home. The next week, I was called by the doctor to come back to the office. There was something in the test. Something was wrong, and she couldn't tell me on the phone. I was in shock. I arrived, and she sat me down at the hospital. "Sarah, I have found something in the test. It's bad news. It looks like you have cancer in your uterus. It could be a mistake, and we want to run another test." I looked at her in shock. "I'm sorry, Sarah."

The next test came back positive also. I was told the next step was surgery. If the cancer came back, I would have to go through chemotherapy. Inside me, I knew I had the Lord. I prayed to Jesus. I believed very much that the Lord could heal me. She told me to go home and tell my family about the cancer. It was important that they knew about this.

I decided never to talk to my children about this cancer, because at that time, they didn't believe in Jesus and didn't have God in their lives. They were living a wild and worldly life. I knew and they knew many people who had died from cancer, even after surgery and chemotherapy. I knew how important I was in their lives. In this world, after God, they had only me.

I knew it didn't matter how they were living, and even when their lifestyle hurt me, I knew that they loved me. I also knew what they went through from childhood. I couldn't make any more hurt for them. So I made the decision to keep that news just between my Daddy God, my lovely Jesus, my dear friend Holy Spirit, and myself. From that moment on, I trusted God. After He had put that calling, vision, dream, and prophecy in my life, cancer could not kill me, but Jesus can kill that cancer.

After a short time, I had surgery. Again they did tests and again they saw cancer. They asked me to return, but this time I didn't go. *Lord, I don't want this. I'll lose my hair; my kids will know. I knew Jesus was the Healer. I will pray for you to heal me.* All of this took one year between the diagnosis, the tests, the surgery, and finally the decision to tell my sons.

One Sunday, I was in church. I had not told my church, for fear it would get back to my sons. I went up for prayer after the sermon. They asked me what I was up there for and I said, "Just pray for me—the Lord knows." Suddenly, I saw a young guy about twenty-two come and put his hand on me during the prayer. I started praying silently in my heart, *Jesus, I know you can heal my cancer.*

Right then, I heard the young guy speak out: "I feel Sarah has cancer and the Lord wants to come right now and heal her cancer." Immediately, everyone opened their eyes and stepped back and looked at the young guy.

Someone said, "Why do you say that? Sarah doesn't have cancer!"

Then I looked at them with tears running down my face. "Yes, I have cancer." They all started to show their feelings and emotions as I told them. "Stop! I feel the Lord's presence. He is here right now, and he wants to heal me." I closed my eyes and opened my arms and said, "Welcome, Lord, you are my Healer." I felt His presence very strongly all over my body as the tears ran down my face, and I had no doubt He was there. He was healing me. People started up again with the questions, but I told them I don't have cancer anymore—I'm healed.

The next day, I went into the hospital and told them, "I want one more test before you do anything else to me." That test came back NO CANCER. They said, "This is complete healing. You can go on normally with your life, even if you want to have a child."

I came home and told my children the whole story. When they learned I had had cancer, I watched their faces fall into shock, but then I told them what Jesus did for me and how much Jesus loves them. This time, they were just quiet. They asked why I didn't tell them about the cancer. I said, "What could you have done?" I told them Jesus was the one who could heal me and He did. Praise His name.

My Bible college was a two-year course, which I finished in one year with intensive effort. As I finished this time, I noticed that I had pain in all my muscles and often had difficulty breathing. I went to visit my doctor, who discovered that I had asthma and fibromyalgia. I couldn't believe it. My muscles began to swell very badly with a great deal of pain. The doctor gave me an inhaler for the asthma and some pain medicine for the fibromyalgia. There was no cure. She also wanted to give me sleeping pills to cope with the stress, but I declined. I knew the Lord would give me peace.

I became very sick. I had to stay home all the time on the couch. I felt very heavy in my body, like a hundred pounds were lying on me. I couldn't go out, not even to church.

During this time, I did take the pain pills but never needed to take the sleeping pills for stress. The Lord gave me peace.

I called some of my friends in the church, hoping they would come to pray for me, visit me, or ask me how they can help. They never came. Some would call to invite me to this church meeting or that church speaker, but I couldn't go. They didn't come to visit me. I lay there remembering when I was working at the salon. How I helped people with their needs, and Lord, where were the people now? Why don't they come and help me?

The Lord started speaking again. He told me not to complain about the weaknesses I saw in other people but to pray over that weakness. He told me that whatever I did to help people in the past, I did it for Him, not Sarah. These words gave me peace.

Love is a commandment from the Lord. We must love each other. Love needs to have action. If someone always says, "I love you," but when they have the chance to show it, they don't, how is that love?

Now the Lord said, "Take your eyes off the people, off your sickness, and focus only on me. When the time comes, I will heal you, but now you have many things to learn. If you have a healthy spirit before me and you have a relationship with me, even if your body is sick or if you die, your sick body stays here on earth and your spirit comes to me. A new body and soul I will give you. Now, if you have healthy body but you aren't spiritually alive, you don't obey me, or live in relationship with me, then if you die, you cannot come to me. I don't mean for you to accept sickness in your body, but don't focus on that sickness. Have faith, pray for your sickness, keep living, and keep praying for other things and people, too."

So every day I started thanking Him for my life, salvation, and family—everything. I prayed for my sickness, too, but I didn't focus on it after that. My focus went back to the Lord as I asked the Holy Spirit to show me where I needed to change my attitude. I was sick almost two and a half years. It was amazing how in that time of focusing on the Lord and how the Holy Spirit taught me things, my relationship with the Lord deepened so much. I felt His presence very much. I prayed a lot. I cried a lot when He showed me things about myself that needed to change, things I had never known about. I felt my body become stronger as I worshipped Him. I could move more as I focused on the Lord.

After a while, I was able to go to church meetings. The preacher said, "Come up for prayer—there is someone here with a problem with asthma." When I heard that, I knew it was me, so I went up for prayer. I received my healing that night.

Never to this day did I ever have a problem with breathing again—no more asthma. I still had the fibromyalgia. The situation in my house was getting worse. My sons were fighting with each other, punching doors, getting angry. I asked some people to pray for them too. There was so much anger and so much hate. They didn't have the Lord. I understood.

One day I sat in the kitchen, looking up into the sky, thinking about all that God had done for us and the plans He had for me. I was smiling, and my middle son Kevin walked into the room and said, "Ah, Mom, look at your life. What's happened to you? You just sit and say *Jesus, Jesus.*"

I looked at him with passion and love and said, "Yes, Kevin, I know. I know. You don't understand now because you don't know who Jesus is, but I know He is your Father. One day, you will know Him too and even serve." Kevin just smirked and left the kitchen.

The days went on as I rested and prayed. One day, I was so down, like I was being squeezed into a box, I felt really paralyzed. I cried to the Lord, "I know you are the true Lord then, even when nothing looks like it's happening. Lord, you said in your Word, 'A bruised reed you will not break—a smoldering spark you will not blow out.' Lord, I see myself like that. I know you can heal my body. I can still do your will in my life. Please give me some relief now."

Later that evening, I went to bed and lay there awake. Now, I don't know how He did it, but He took me to heaven. I left the earth. Someone took me into heaven. I saw I was flying, and under me was the ocean, shining like crystal. But at that moment, I felt I was before the throne of God. I could feel the life force, joy, and pleasure flowing through every cell of my being. This was something I had never experienced or even imagined before. I cried out to God, "How I understand that part of your work now. You say, 'I talk to you of earthly things and you don't understand.' How can I talk to you of heavenly things?" Now I was suddenly back on my bed … still awake.

That feeling of life and pleasure that was inside my body was still with me. And it stayed with me, exactly as it was before the throne of God for one whole week. I thought a lot about, *Wow, what a great and pleasurable time it will be when we go to the Lord.* No suffering or pain today can even compare to what is ahead of us with Jesus, in heaven.

I am still faced with fibromyalgia and the pain of it at this time. Unable to get out and around .

At this time, my three boys were still living with me, but they were not living for the Lord. As I mentioned previously, when I sold my salon, I used the money I had to plant seeds into the lives of people I felt I was supposed to, along with the care of my children and myself. Because I was no longer working, I was faced with very limited finances that were quickly running out.

I spent a lot of time in my kitchen, as many moms do, for reasons we all know. I would sit at my favorite place by the window. I love the light that shines through a big, beautiful window. As I was sitting there drinking my coffee, enjoying my prayer time with the Lord, a storm arose. This storm was actually my son, Kevin. He was very upset over something trivial in his room or about his room. His apparent rage was very unsettling to me, and the peace I was experiencing just moments before was now a rage. I will say the rage was only one-sided. This was not always the case before Jesus was Lord of my life. At that time, this would have been two-sided and would have ended with two very angry, upset people with no resolve.

The Lord spoke to me and instructed me to deal patiently with my boys and to show them "His love." This is what I did to Kevin that day. I said to him, "I love you, Kevin. I don't know what is wrong, but I love you." He was upset that I was smiling and at first interpreted it as smiling in a ridiculing way. I explained to him that my smile was sincere and a joy I had from the Lord, re-affirming my love for him. He stormed away. I knew at that time the Lord had helped me to stay calm because of His strength and peace in me.

Much to my surprise, Kevin came back into the kitchen and hugged me. "Mom, I don't know what's happening to me. I am sorry." This was such a blessing to me to see and experience God's faithfulness to answer my prayers. I was very grateful to the Holy Spirit's instruction to me about how to lead my children to Him not by always badgering them about serving Him going to church, etc. But the Holy Spirit instructed me to show them by the sacrifice of my own life separated unto Him that no matter what, I was to show them the love of the Lord by example and not by mere words.

I will be honest with you: at this time, I was very upset. In my feelings, I wanted to act and react differently from the way my Lord would have wanted. But I knew I was not to go by my feelings, but I was to be obedient to the Lord and act the way that would be becoming of Him, to show His love.

We cannot win a battle sword to sword. The enemy is overcome by God's love, and He had done a work in my life. I had to continue to trust Him and that He would continue to help me trust Him. God's promise to me was that someday my children also would accept Him as their Lord and Savior.

One evening, my oldest son Cyrus was very sad about something regarding one of his friends. Because he was so sad, I went in to see him in his room and wrapped my arms around him, as any mom would do. I began to talk with him and apologize if I said anything that hurt him before Jesus came into my life. Cyrus was very gracious and forgiving to me. He shared with me that he chose to do the right things because he didn't want to hurt me, because of his love and respect for me. I was very blessed and I felt very good when I heard this from him.

One afternoon, my youngest son Alex, who at this time was in high school, came home from school. As he stood in the doorway with his friend, I could see that the side of his face had been badly beaten and bruised. He immediately began to defend the man who did this to him, because he was afraid of how upset I would be. He always knew I was very protective of my boys. He did this even before I could ask, "Who did this to you?" He began to say this man might have had problems at home or a new baby or something, still defending him. Alex and his friend began simultaneously and very excitedly to tell the story.

As the story was told to me, Alex was through with his theatre/drama class, and the next class had already begun. Alex remembered that he had forgotten something in that class, so he stepped back in, and much to his surprise and to the surprise of many others, his drama teacher grabbed him and proceeded to kick him repeatedly. In our country of Sweden, everyone knows that no matter what the offense, an adult is never ever allowed to strike a minor. Alex's friend began to warn that Kevin, Alex's older brother whom everyone knew, was a very well-known and feared gang leader. Alex was now on his way to take matters into his own hands. The school, finding this out, called the police. In fear of the teacher's safety, they proceeded to lock the teacher in a room away from Kevin. The police and Kevin arrived at the same time, so Kevin was unable to intervene. Alex's friend encouraged me to sue this man for lots of money because he was clearly at fault and guilty of attacking Alex, who was underage. The decision was up to me. What would I do?

Meanwhile, Kevin and Cyrus came home, very upset about what happened to their brother. I begged them, even made them promise to let me deal with this in my own way. They reluctantly listened but gave me their word nevertheless. The school called me the very next day to come to a meeting. I think they were anxious to see what I would do. They knew this could mean a lot of bad publicity for their school and a jail sentence with huge liability fines for their teacher. I went to this meeting. In the hallway, I realized I would come face to face with my son's attacker, his teacher. How ironic that someone who is to watch over and teach would do this. He approached with an outstretched hand, obviously realizing that he was "guilty as charged." What fate would—or I should say *could*—await him from this heinous act of violence against my youngest son? I did outstretch my hand with a stronger grasp than should be expected from a woman of my size, letting him know my feelings by my handshake and the obvious look in my eyes, and I will add the tone of my voice. I proceeded to tell him that I am not afraid of the government or of jail or anything. "If it were not for Jesus in my life, I would kill you myself," I said, "for what you have done to my son. You have no idea what I have gone through to bring my children here to this country to protect them from their abusive father and to try to give them a better life." I loosened my grasp and backed away as the principal realized my presence and was ready to begin the meeting. We proceeded into another room, and the principal, the teacher, my son, and I sat around a table.

The principal began the meeting. Much to my amazement, the principal— well knowing what had happened—began to downplay the whole incident, making it look much less than it was. In the meantime, my son sat next to me with his face badly swollen and bruised. How could the principal make this out to be less than it was? I proceeded to tell her that although I was not from this country, I still knew the laws. I really didn't appreciate her lackadaisical attitude about what happened to my son. I knew the police had many witnesses who knew what was done to my son. She had to be reminded, and I did remind her that I knew this was a crime, one in which we were clearly in the right and they were in the wrong. When she saw I was not afraid but clearly knew my rights as a parent and clearly knew the rights regarding this incident, she changed her attitude.

I proceeded to tell her I knew that I could put the teacher in jail and sue him for a lot of money. I proceeded to tell the teacher that what he had done was wrong; I knew my rights and could easily exercise them. I told him that he should change his life and that I was going to forgive him and told him that Jesus loved him. They were both stunned and surprised by my final reaction to this whole situation. I ended this meeting with hugs to both the teacher and the principal.

When I got home, my son's friend and many of mine who had heard what had happened began many times over to ask me, "What have you done? You could sue him and get a lot of money." So many thoughts then came into my mind, because I was still sickly and without any income. Oh, how I could have used that money in so many ways and for so many things!

But I knew most importantly I was doing what was right before the Lord. Maybe they have never heard about Jesus; maybe by my act of love and forgiveness to my son's offender, I could plant seeds into that man's life and the principal's life. I knew what was right before my Lord, and doing that was more important to me.

I had been dealing with a very serious muscle illness called fibromyalgia for about a year and a half. I had been to many doctors and, never getting a good report, realized the seriousness of my condition, with nowhere else to turn and no hope for recovery. I was referred to the Rehabilitation Center, a center of specialized doctors who could now give me a recommendation to have what we call in Sweden "early retirement," which would ensure me a monthly check for the disability that I had. After waiting more than a year, I finally received in the mail my chance to go to this center.

The day before my appointment at the center began like any other. It came, and evening was upon me, just like any other. The only thing different about this day was that earlier, I had been reading a book about how God had healed someone, and I began to think back about how the Lord had previously healed me of cancer and asthma. As I sat upon my bed, I began to worship the Lord in tongues and ask Him to heal my fibromyalgia. It had left me with very painful and swollen muscles, the inability to move around freely, along with a bodily "heaviness" that also accompanied this condition. I was also on pain medication. I inquired of Him this night and believed Him to heal me, as He did the man in the book, and as He had done twice before of my very serious diseases.

My future report of fibromyalgia was inevitably going to be paralysis. I didn't want that. About an hour or so into my worship, I began to feel a sensation of what felt like warm oil being poured over my body. Unknown to me, I was being healed. I could feel that the pain and swelling were gone, along with the heaviness. I felt as though I was burning with no fire. Could it be I was healed? Yes, I was! That moment, I knew I had definitely received my healing. Now I was really excited and continued to worship the Lord for about another hour. Then I heard a voice, which I quickly recognized as the enemy's, saying, "You didn't really get healed; you're just thinking that." Just as quickly, I rebuked the evil one who had tried to convince me that the Lord had not healed me. Once again he tried, and I rebuked him again. I continued to remind him that I knew I was healed and the victory was mine.

The day after I was healed was the day I was scheduled to go to the Rehabilitation Center. I asked myself, "Should I go or not?" I knew I was healed, but the enemy continued to try to make me believe I was not really healed by bringing back the same symptoms of the disease, as well as the thoughts that maybe I really wasn't healed or maybe it would come back. I didn't want to go to the center and lie. Not knowing what to do, I contacted a very godly woman whom I respected. She told me I should go to the center because I had had the illness for quite some time. So I went.

The chief of the doctors checked me out very thoroughly and with great seriousness. They had to be sure I was telling the truth, because they had to give the okay if I truly was sick that I could receive monthly checks from the insurance company for the rest of my life. How nice it would be to receive checks for the rest of my life! I was a single mom, and even three or four days later, the enemy continued to try to make me believe that I wasn't healed. This battle in my mind continued ... was I—wasn't I? So many voices.

I also continued to go back to the center a couple more times. As time went on, I could not deny what happened to me that night, no matter what my body felt like at times. Someone told me how I could benefit from the monthly checks, in case I was wrong about my healing. I knew that no one—not even this person who loved me and cared so much for me—could understand what had happened to me. I realized at that time, as much as I appreciated advice, I had to obey what I believe the Lord was teaching me through this. As wonderful and necessary as it is to get godly counsel and advice, I still had to obey the Holy Spirit in my heart and what I knew as only I could what truly happened in my body that night. I had to acknowledge that I truly was healed. There would be no monthly checks, but better than that, no fibromyalgia. The chief doctor even called me and left the door open for me to come back; another temptation to doubt. I now had chosen to stand on the true fact that no matter what, the Lord had healed me.

I hung up the phone and began to praise the Lord. I never returned to the center and have been symptom-free since 2003. At this time, my eldest son Cyrus had moved out on his own into an efficiency apartment.

As I was praying one day, I was talking to the Lord, telling Him that I have finished Bible college, sold my salon, how He has healed my fibromyalgia, and how much He has taught me through all of that. I asked Him, "Now, what do you want me to do, Lord?"

As I continued to pray, the Lord said, "Now is the time I want you to go to the United States." As I inquired of the Lord why I would go there—because it's a big country and I don't know anyone there—a woman's face came to me, someone I had met at a Christian conference in Florida in 2000. After that year I'd had no contact with her.

I said to the Lord, "How can I just call her?"

The Lord answered, "Just call her and you will see."

I searched all of my old business cards to try to find this woman, whose picture the Lord brought before me and He wanted me to call. I found it and called the number on the card. This woman, whose name is Sally, was not there. Unfortunately, she had since been divorced from her husband, with whom I was now on the phone. It just so happened that this man handed the phone to his daughter, who was there. She proceeded to tell me where her mother was. She gave me her new phone number.

So I called Sally. At first, she wasn't sure who I was, so I explained how the Lord had told me to call her. She was very excited, because she had just prayed that God would send someone to help her with her parents. Her father, who was seriously ill, had caretakers during the day but no one to stay with them at night. Her elderly mom was afraid at night. There was even a room available for me to stay in at their home. Her sister Mary, who lived with her parents, had just gotten a job in New York. This would be so perfect for me and also for this family, who were praying and believing in God to send someone to live with her parents.

Sally said to just buy a ticket and come. The Lord had previously told me to sell my home and possessions. Since I was now going to the USA, I knew I had to put my home on the market. At this time, the market for selling homes was really bad. I was already two months in debt to my neighbors, because after selling my salon, I had no more income coming in. So I put my house on the market, gave away many of my possessions to people in need, and gave Cyrus what would fit into his efficiency apartment.

Since I was now going to move, Kevin and Alex moved into their brother's efficiency apartment. Miraculously—and I will say again, miraculously—my home sold within one month. No one could believe it. From the sale of my home, I had to pay off the house, all my debts, and some back taxes. I was so dependent on my children and they on me. This move would be very hard. How could I leave them? None of my children was saved, and they were living very worldly and wild lives. This would be very hard for me. But I also knew I had to obey the Lord and His promise to me that He would take care of my children. He said to me, "Don't worry, I will take care of them."

So I bought my ticket and arrived in Miami in June 2003. Sally greeted me at the airport with flowers. She was very excited. I also gave her a nice gold necklace as a gift. We proceeded to her parents' home, and I talked with them. So here I was; I spent my first night. Her sister Mary had left only two days before for her new job in New York.

Upon awakening the next day, to our surprise, we found out that her sister Mary would be coming back from New York, because the job wasn't what she expected. So, she came back and I continued to stay there at Sally's parents' home for about two more weeks. I began to feel uncomfortable in an environment with so much sickness, with me having been sick for so long. They never said anything, but I knew I wasn't needed any longer because the sister was now home and could take over. I am very excited to say that the Lord did use me to lead Mary to Him because she was not saved before I came.

Within the two weeks that I was there, I remembered an Iranian pastor that I knew lived in Tulsa, Oklahoma. I contacted him and told him I wanted to learn more English and possibly go to Bible college. He suggested Oral Roberts University.

I bought a ticket to go to Tulsa with some of the money I had left from the sale of my home. My flight wasn't to leave for another week, so I contacted the pastor in Miami who had the Christian conference where Sally and I had met. I told him my situation, and he said that I could stay with him and his wife. So I went to stay with them for my last week.

While I was there, I met a single girl named Ellen from their church. We instantly became friends. She said she wanted to take me to the beach, which sounded very refreshing to me after all I had been through so far.

She also said that the Lord told her that what she would be doing for me, she was doing for the Lord. She graciously invited me to spend my last week at her home. This was a great idea, because although the pastor and his wife invited me to stay with them, they were very busy planning their daughter's wedding. Therefore, this would be a very good move. Ellen had her own business inside her home, so we were able to spend a lot of time together that week. When she took me to the airport, she said that if I didn't feel comfortable in Tulsa, her home was always open to me to return to. I thanked her and got on the plane headed for Tulsa.

When I arrived in Tulsa, the pastor and his wife picked me up at the airport and took me to their home. The pastor shared with me about a man from his church, Paul, who trained as an engineer and now owned a Taco Bell. He was dependable, a believer, and a good man for me to marry. I told him I didn't come to marry. He insisted for me to stay open to the idea because I had said for so many years I was single and that is why it's hard for me to think about this. I did admit that I didn't feel called to be single.

Later we met for a dinner. Paul invited the pastor and his wife to meet at his brother's house, and we had a really nice meal. It was a beautiful home. Paul was pleasant and seemed normal, but I didn't feel anything out of the ordinary for him. By the pastor's suggestion, Paul and I met for lunch and coffee. We talked about many things: the future, our likes and dislikes, as we got to know each other. He said he felt that I was the one for him and that we should marry. He proposed and I told him that I needed time to think. I called my sister, who said, "Sarah, if he's a good man, just do it. You're getting older. I want this for you. I want for you to be settled and married to a good man in your life." As she said this, I remembered my mother's wishes for me—always to be married and settled with a good man. I believe that as she spoke to me about this, my mom's spirit had somehow been passed on to my sister.

My next call was to my sons. I explained that this man—a good, believing man, stable financially, selected by the pastor—wants to marry me. I asked them what they thought. Each of my sons felt the same way. They said, "Mom, it's time to think about yourself. If you want this marriage, please do it!" Well, I was relieved by my sons' response. There was nothing to overcome with them. They were for me marrying the man of my choice.

At this time, I was also considering Bible college and Oral Roberts University. One day, I went over to the school and inquired about starting classes. They explained to me about the fees, and I realized the cost was too much for me. I didn't have that kind of money. I had attended two years of Bible college in Sweden, and I just didn't see a reason or a way to pay such a large amount of money for this school.

Pastor and friends asked about what I had decided about school. I said, "The cost is too high. I cannot attend this school, but one day I will come back and preach in Oral Roberts University." Ha! I really believed this, too!

I continued meeting with Paul, talking over dinners. I know he wanted marriage with me. My pastor began to worry that Paul would be hurt if I didn't make a decision soon. He asked that I take the next two days to really pray about it and make my decision. Wow! During the next two days, I was so full of questions for God. "Is this the one? Lord, you know how I always held a dream in my heart—a romantic dream for true love. Paul is a good man, a believer, and has a normal job. Do you want me to settle down with Paul? Is this really your will, Lord?"

The next day, I again called home to Sweden. My middle son, Kevin—the tough guy—answered the phone. Though Kevin had not received Jesus in his heart at this time, he spoke to me with passion. I admitted to Kevin that I was struggling with this decision. Kevin began to remind me of what was important. "Mom, don't think about anything else but this: remember how you were forced to marry Dad when you didn't love him? Remember, you've always wanted true love, romance, and the 'real deal'? Mom, this is what I want you to do right now: close your eyes and think about that dream of romance. Can you see that dream with this man? Can you really love him? If you don't see it with him, please, Mom, don't do it!"

I hung up the phone and had such joy in my heart. My son really was thinking about my feelings, my heart, and what I wanted. That felt very good.

The next day, Paul picked me up for coffee and "the decision." I was in his car and suddenly thought about it. How many times had I been proposed to in the past? How many times had I said no? How tired I was of this! I am a godly woman; I can be married and serve the Lord. This is my special dream, so why should I say no to him?

As we rode along in the car, I saw the anticipation on his face for my answer. We rode in silence. He knew I was preparing to give him my answer. The next minute, I heard myself saying, "Okay, I will marry you!"

Paul was so happy. He reached over and took my hand and lifted it to kiss it. This was our first kiss, just a respectful kiss to my hand as he drove. As he did this, wow, I felt it—something was not right. There was absolutely no connection. There was not the least bit of anything that I had expected. Reflexes made me pull my hand back so quickly that I shocked him. He looked over at me and asked me in shock, "Sarah, what's wrong?"

I looked over at him, and the words came spilling out. "No, Paul, I can't do this. It's not right. We aren't right for each other." That was the truth. He was heartbroken and confused. I felt very bad. We went on to the pastor's house and broke the news to everyone who was there. They were sure this was going to happen. After all, he was such a great situation for me. How could I have said no? But there was no way I could marry someone without that connection—that love. Also, it wasn't only me saying no, because deep in my heart, I knew it wasn't just my feeling about not being connected to this man; it was not the Lord's will. For me to marry him, it was so more than just *my* decision.

After that, I didn't feel free to stay with that pastor, his wife, and family any longer. I was no longer welcome because I hadn't taken their advice. I felt I had to leave their house, but I still had a month and a half left on my visa. I still had not found the purpose of why the Lord brought me to the United States.

Then I remembered Ellen in Florida. She had taken me to the Miami airport to come to Tulsa and said if I wanted to come back to her house, I was welcome. She said what the Lord told her what she would do for me, she would be doing for the Lord. I called her and explained my awkward situation. She assured me that I did the right thing and I should come and stay with her for the last month and a half of my visa. I was very thankful to the Lord and to her, and I bought my ticket to Miami.

I arrived at the airport, and Ellen brought me to her home. She said these words to me: "Where I go, you will go. Where I live, you live. What I eat, you will eat." We became very close friends. The Lord began to use each of us for the other. We really ministered to each other. She had received the Lord the exact same year I did. At that time, she had been trying to live a clean life before the Lord, as she waited on the Lord's timing for marriage. Now she is married to a pastor.

Ellen had her office in her apartment and had a swimming pool out front. Every day I swam in that pool, it was very refreshing. To stay there was such a blessing after going through the many things I had gone through.

Ellen's job was selling computer parts to other countries. She had one partner. He was a Christian and a married man with three children.

One day, Ellen took me with her to one of the factories she bought computer parts from. It was a very big one. Ellen introduced me to the owner, and we began to talk. She told the factory owner who I was, about my life, and that I lived with her now. As the conversation progressed, I began to share with that man about Jesus. I told him how I was Muslim and received the Lord. I shared about my relationship with Jesus. This man was a very serious Orthodox Christian. When I was finished, he offered to train me to sell computer parts to other countries, just like Ellen did. He said, "You can work for me. Apply for a visa and stay here. Please come for lunch and meet my wife tomorrow."

Ellen and I went back to the car after our meeting with the factory owner. She started telling me how amazing this invitation was. "Sarah," she said, "in all the times I've met with this man, he has never said anything to me as a person. It has always been strictly business. This is amazing that he has invited us out to lunch and that we will meet his wife."

The next day, we met him and his wife at a restaurant. She was very pleasant and friendly as he told her about his plan to train and employ me. He also could assist with his lawyers to get a working visa. Wow! It was unbelievable. I told him I would have to think it over. As I looked over this huge opportunity, it was very tempting: a great job in Florida, the money, an interesting life in the warm sunshine. This really called out to me.

Ellen started asking me what I was going to do. I think she was looking at me and wondering if I was really going to follow what God called me to do. She knew my story, and I believe she wanted to know if I was telling the truth about who I was now with Jesus or if I would jump at things the world was offering me. Whatever she was thinking at that time, I'm not sure, but this was not about her or even about me; this was really about the Lord's will. I knew this much: God didn't say, "Go to Florida and I will give you a great job." So, the decision became clear. I asked Ellen to say to the factory owner, "Thank you so much for your generous job offer, but I am not interested in accepting it." It was not for me; I am the Lord's servant and He has other purposes in my life.

I had about a week before my visa ran out, and then I would return to Sweden. I still didn't see God's purpose for this trip that I just took to the United States. That afternoon, I went up before the Lord. I went into the bed room, closed the door, and got down on my knees. "Oh, Lord, you've brought me through so much. You saved me, healed my sickness, told me to sell all I had and serve you 100 percent. I heard you say to come to the United States. Now I've had a marriage proposal from someone I knew wasn't right for me. I was offered a wonderful job, but I know you didn't bring me here just to get another job. Lord, did I misunderstand you somewhere along the line? Oh, God, I have one week left. If nothing happens during this week, I will return to Sweden and not come back to the U.S. I will understand this whole trip was my idea, not yours, and that I really did misunderstand you. Lord, I cannot do anything in this week by my power. This week I give to you; whatever you want, just do it."

After praying, I got up off my knees and left that room. I didn't tell Ellen or anyone about what I prayed. That night, I slept.

In the morning, Ellen rose earlier than me to prepare for her work as usual. As I lay there, Ellen came into my room excitedly. "Sarah, Sarah, wake up. I have good news for you."

I woke up startled. "What's happened, Ellen?"

"You remember you told your testimony for my business partner? Today, he just came and said that the Lord put into his heart to start a non-profit organization to help the churches in poor countries. Sarah, he wants to hire you as a missionary to go to the countries and come back and report on their needs. Thomas told me to go and wake you, Sarah. He said, 'Her time is short and I want to take her to a lawyer now who can arrange all of this and set Sarah up as our non-profit missionary worker.'"

I was still sleepy as I heard this. For a minute, I thought it might be a dream. But no, this was really happening. My dear, sweet Jesus heard my prayer last night.

He Read My Letter

I got up, got ready, and went with Thomas and Ellen to a very excellent lawyer. The lawyer said that since I had such a short time left on my visa, I should return to Sweden and come back to the United States again as soon as I could. Then she would begin working on my paperwork to make me a non-profit missionary worker for this organization that they would be setting up. She told Thomas that he needed to get all the things done to set up this organization before they brought me back to her.

We returned to Ellen's apartment, and I began to think back on everything that had happened to me on this trip. I remembered the days that I would walk around the lake by Ellen's house. How many wonderful things happened as I met people walking each day! Some would stop me, and we began to recognize each and would say hello. We would talk. They shared their feelings and needs. I was able to share Jesus with some of them and even pray for many of them. It was such a good time each day. Each day was a new journey into the hearts of God's people. Some of them were new believers, some battling unforgiveness, and one young person just came up to me to say that he saw a kind of light around me. I shared with him that it was Jesus. One lady invited me to her church after I shared my testimony with her at that lake.

One day, a man around fifty years old was biking on the path at the lake. I was walking and talking to my Heavenly Father, unaware of what was happening around me. This man came up to me and said, "Excuse me, miss, I've seen you walking and you are so focused. You seem to be in another place. How is it you meditate like that?" I think he thought I was into new age meditation. But I told him I was talking to my Heavenly Father. He wanted to know more, and I told him that I used to be Muslim and that I believe in Jesus now. Then I shared my testimony with him and told him what I was doing here. After that I asked him, "How about you? What are you doing? Do you live here?" He said he was from New Mexico, where he worked as a lawyer. Now he was here on vacation.

I asked him, "Do you believe in Jesus?" He said he had heard of Jesus but that he wasn't one to go to church or follow Jesus.

I said, "I'm so sorry that you don't." Right then, I felt the Lord tell me to ask him if I could pray for him about anything. I asked him, "Sir, is there anything specific in your life that you can't handle, that you cannot fix?

If you want, I can pray for that, and I know Jesus can take care of that for you through his Holy Spirit."

In that quiet moment, he looked me in the eyes and said, "Well, um, for many years I've had a problem with my wife. Now I have a lot of bitterness in my heart for her, and I cannot fix that. Do you think your Jesus can fix that?"

I looked him straight in the eyes and said, "Yes, He can—just believe."

Next, I put my hand on his head, and in my broken English, I began to pray for that lawyer man. Suddenly I felt the Holy Spirit come so strongly over his heart, and the tears started running down his face. I believe this was his first experience with God's love.

After I finished praying, his eyes were red from the tears, and he said, "I don't know what's happened, but it's strange, I feel much better."

I told him, "I'm finishing with my prayer and my part, but I think your part is just beginning. Your relationship with Jesus can start now if you want that." I said good-bye to that man and never saw him again.

Two days before my return flight to Sweden, Ellen and Thomas and I were sitting after work, discussing the non-profit organization. We prayed, and Thomas said the non-profit organization would take some time to be up and running. He wanted to start out small with what he had now, and Ellen wanted to be part of this too. Then he left.

After dinner, Ellen and I were in prayer about how to start the ministry now with what we had and where to start. The Spirit of the Lord came over us very strongly, and Ellen and I both began to cry. I started saying, "Armenia, Armenia," without even thinking about Armenia.

Ellen looked at me and asked, "Sarah, why Armenia? Do you know someone there?"

My thoughts went back to the time in Sweden when I was very sick and a pastor had come from the Armenian church. He shared about his life back in Armenia and how the people there had such a great big heart for the Lord. He shared how the Holy Spirit was being poured out so much upon the church there and about how very poor the people in that country were. As he spoke that night at our church meeting, I was touched and moved in a way I still remember to this day. I had been sick, wasn't working, and didn't have much money to give, but what I had that night, I gave to that man to give to his people. My wish at that moment was that one day I would go to that country and the people there would pray for me.

When I shared this memory with Ellen and later Thomas, they were in total agreement. I would be returning to Sweden, and from there I could visit Armenia. I would return to Sweden and from there come back to Florida to report on the needs of that church in Armenia.

The time came for me to return to Sweden with a mission to do for the Lord. I was happy, and happy to see my boys. They didn't believe in Jesus yet, but I felt that he was beginning to teach them things in a way they could understand. I was very proud of Cyrus. He had wanted an apartment of his own, and now he had let his brothers live with him too. I was very thankful to God for his life, for that great big heart of his. My three sons didn't know Jesus yet, but He knew them. I know that He gave me a promise that not only would they know him someday, but they would serve. Him

Now I was also staying at Cyrus's apartment. Cyrus slept on the kitchen floor with the door closed. He gave his bed to Kevin, I slept on the couch, and Alex slept on the floor. It was crazy. One day we had our big house with our private bedrooms with nice waterbeds, but there was a lot of fighting in that house. Now here we were in an efficiency apartment, sleeping on the floors, and no one complained.

I started asking around at the church about that pastor from Armenia. I got his number, called him, and shared with him about our vision. The pastor warmly received my vision and said, "Oh, Sister Sarah, when you are ready to come and you have your ticket, just call, let me know the day and time, and I'll come to the airport and pick you up."

My first mission trip was about to happen. I was happy and excited to go, but I was very surprised when I heard the Lord say, "Take Kevin with you, the stormy one." Now, Kevin's life at this time was 100 percent worldly and wild. Of all my boys, he was the most critical of my faith in Jesus. This was not going to be a vacation. We were going to a poor country. I didn't know what we would face concerning food, a place to stay, and everything else. For me alone, it was okay no matter what, because I was there to serve the Lord. But for Kevin, I was scared for him. He could say or do something crazy in front of godly people and embarrass "Sister Sarah." I told the Lord, "Okay, Lord, I will invite him, but I cannot force him to come. If you want him to come, then you must do it."

The next day, I did it: I invited Kevin to go to Armenia with me. He looked at me and said, "Why are you going to Armenia?" I told him the Lord put it in my heart. He said, "Okay." Wow, I couldn't believe what I just heard.

I remembered then what the Lord taught me a long time ago: the things that are impossible for us are possible with Him. This I knew, but wow, with some people, especially Kevin, he was so wild and worldly. I bought two tickets to Armenia. I was very excited at the same time. I called the pastor in Armenia and gave him the date and time we would be arriving. He would be there to pick us up when we arrived.

The day came for us to go to Armenia. The pastor picked us up, as he said he would. It was winter and it was very, very cold. We were used to this, because winters in Sweden were also very cold. Of course, once inside your home with heat and other amenities to keep you warm, the winter cold was not a problem. We found that to be different at this home in Armenia. Kevin and I spent a very long night being colder than we'd ever been and almost unable to stand it. The only heater they had was in the middle of their main living area. Without proper bedding and with very little heat, we almost froze. My dear son, who was usually very rough around the edges, didn't say a word but became very tender and caring. Where was my old Kevin? This surprised even me. Where was the usual outburst that he usually portrayed when things didn't go his way?

We awoke the next morning and spoke to the pastor about helping to find us an apartment. He helped us. We were, of course, excited and it had heat. That was wonderful because we would be there for ten days. In that time, we would visit many different churches where I would speak and share Scriptures the Lord put in my heart and give my testimony. I would talk to the people about what their needs were and then make a report. At one of the churches we visited, there were between 250 and 300 people attending a church service at which I was the scheduled speaker. The power of God was so strong during the meeting even the power to heal.

I laid hands on many people, and even they testified of their healings. My son Kevin watched in utter amazement. He probably thought, *What is happening? What is my mom doing? This is my mom; the person I even at times had ridiculed her faith, the very faith that God is now using to help so many people?* After that, he said not one word. I was able to minister to many people. I met so many poor people, some Christian and some not. I was very excited because I was able to help them not only spiritually, but I was able to give them financial help as well out of my own substance.

It amazed me that even in such poverty, the Christian people had the joy of the Lord. I want to mention that on occasion, we were able to meet Armenian people who were unable to speak a word of English, but when they would praise the Lord in tongues, they would suddenly be speaking fluent English as their prayer language. Another did so in fluent French. This amazed Kevin so much that he even recorded their prayer language on his phone.

After visiting many churches in Armenia and assessing their needs, my reports were done. We headed first back to Sweden, where I would stop home (Cyrus's efficiency apartment) where I lived with my three sons, before heading back to Florida. One night, before I had fallen asleep, I was reflecting back on the time when I had first met this Armenian pastor when he was in Sweden. I remembered how he used to talk about the Armenian people and how the power of God would come when they prayed, and I remember thinking how I would love for the Armenian people to pray for me. I was surprised at how God worked this so that I was the one going to Armenia and praying for them.

After returning home, Kevin returned to his very wild and worldly lifestyle, even after witnessing everything in Armenia.

I remained in Sweden for two weeks, spending time with my children. Then I went on to Florida and reported back to Ellen and Thomas all the needs of the churches and what was happening there. After we talked it over, we sent money to the different churches. While I was waiting for Ellen and Thomas to register and to finish all the paperwork and the Web site for their non-profit organization, I began to attend Miami-Dade College. This whole process of starting and establishing the non-profit organization took two years. In that time, I would go back and forth to Sweden and attend college.

Right before we were about to get the certificate for the non-profit organization after two years of so much work and paperwork, Thomas decided to move out of the state. Elaine said, "I cannot do this alone."

Now, there I was in this alone. I said, "Okay, Lord, they both gave up. I know I am not dependent on people. I am dependent on you. I know you called me to be an evangelist, and I want to know what is your next step for me."

As mentioned previously, after we received the certificate for the non-profit organization, I was to take it to my lawyer so that I could now be a certified non-profit organizational missionary worker. But since Thomas and Ellen were no longer involved or staying to the finish, how could I finish this phase of what we had started? I inquired of the Lord, especially about what I was supposed to do now.

Then the Lord opened a door for me in Ohio, and I went there. From there, I went to different places in different countries. I will say at this point in my life I had no more money from the sale of my home. Each time before I traveled, the Lord would give me a vision and confirmation for a certain country. I would obey the Lord, knowing that He would provide for me for every need.

One of my studies in college was the role of a marriage counselor. I realized the Lord had given me a special anointing. I saw how strong the gift was. It was so supernatural that even I knew it was much more than just the knowledge I acquired from college. I was even able to pray with many couples. I could see the change in their lives, a change that only the power of God could have done, sometimes astounding even me. I was very happy and thankful that the Lord would use me in this way, that through His Holy Spirit in my life, he has graced me in different areas to be able to be used by Him to minister help and healing in whatever capacity He chooses for me. I am His willing servant.

In the year 2008, a pastor from Sweden encouraged me to attend a five-month course for missionary teaching in Dallas, Texas. It was a very intense study for those ready and willing to serve the Lord in some capacity on the mission field. Every week, we were taught by very anointed and dedicated leaders from different states in the field of missionary service. I learned much from this experience. Every teacher who would come would teach about a specific area about God.

One day, we had a teacher who spoke to us about how the things that have happened to us—either in our past or through generational curses—could be passed down to us and affect us now in our lives, naturally or spiritually.

Many people have shame, guilt, and anger because of what has happened to them. He said he wanted to pray for each of us individually for healing and deliverance. So, when it was my turn, I went with him and another woman teacher. They prayed for me. As I mentioned earlier in my book, I had not only been molested as a young child but was also raped while in Turkey. I did not reveal that to these two teachers; I just told them to pray for me to be delivered from all the curses or effects of my past. I felt a very strong presence of the Lord as they prayed for me. I cried a lot, also feeling that now I was free from all the effects of my past.

After every speaker, our teacher would announce who the next speaker would be for us. She told us about the couple from South Africa who would be here to teach us about deliverance and even pray for us. I couldn't believe I did this, but I began to complain. I, who had a love for God and always wanted to learn more. I was so hungry for the Word of God that I found the teacher and other students looking at me, I think stunned at my complaining attitude. "Why do we have to be delivered again? We already were taught this and even prayed for." Speaking to the teacher I said, "Don't you believe we were already delivered? Where is your faith?"

At that moment, I still didn't understand why, even though I had been prayed for, why did I still have shame and fear? Why could I not tell anyone about what had happened to me? I had never ever told anyone about the molestation or rape. I didn't tell my family or even my closest friends, never anyone. It was just between God and me. Even when you're a small child, you don't want this. You are innocent; you don't even know sometimes what the perpetrator is doing to you. In the case of rape, the name is given because you have been forced against your will in this act. And why when you've been molested or raped does the victim have to deal with such shame and fear and guilt over an act that they were forced into? Why? Why would the victim feel these things? What causes you to feel this way? When you were the innocent one, why do we feel we cannot tell? The shame and guilt should be on the people who do these things to us, not on the innocent victims. If only those people who do such heinous and unspeakable things could know how the few moments of having to satisfy their flesh and have what they think is pleasure, how drastically they can cause such a lifetime of suffering and pain to their victims. You must know there are spirits behind all of those feelings of shame, disappointment, anger, and fear to tell.

There are men and women alike who can share in what I have been through. It doesn't matter if you were a Christian or not, you must know that the spirits behind these things that happened to you can affect many areas of your life. You can be prayed for and delivered from them. You must know—and I say this strongly to you—you must tell someone about what has happened to you and let him or her pray specifically about what has happened to you. It is not enough to just pray for something in general. And when you do this, you will be truly set free and you will also feel free from all of the shame, fear, anger, and guilt. You do not have to be afraid to tell your testimony anymore, because it was not your fault.

The next scheduled speakers were a couple from South Africa. They were going to talk specifically about that, although we were Christians and very anointed by the Lord to do His work. There were some who can still have strongholds or bondages in their lives from their past that they needed to be healed and delivered from. One of our leaders, whose name was Susan, was telling us that before the next teachers would speak to us, she wanted to share something with us that she had never shared with her class before. She wasn't sure why she was doing it, but she felt very strongly that the Lord wanted her to tell her testimony. When she was a young girl, she had been repeatedly sexually abused by one of her family members. The whole class listened very intently as she shared her testimony. I listened closely.

But then something came over me, and I began to cry uncontrollably, and I could feel anger begin to rise up inside of me. Why was I crying? Why was I feeling this way? They already prayed for me, and I have been delivered from the pain of my past. I didn't want anyone to see how I was now feeling out of control with my emotions, so I stormed out of the classroom. Susan followed after me, and I cried as she tried to comfort me.

She said, "Sarah, let this couple pray for you; they can help." So that evening, this South African couple invited all of us in the classroom to a meeting in which we were all instructed to form a circle. Then they announced that they wanted anyone who had been sexually abused to come forward for prayer. The others could watch and learn how to deal with this type of need in someone's life and how to properly pray for him or her. As we began to praise and worship I became so touched by the Lord, I could not stop crying. They had announced for anyone to come forth who wanted prayer for sexual abuse. It was very hard for me. I had never told a single soul about what had happened to me.

But I have learned that although it is very hard, we have to also choose to be free. So I put one foot in front of the other, and for the first time, I came forward. I sat down in a chair and proceeded to tell them about my molestation and rape. As I spoke these words, I could feel them place their hands on my head and pray. I could feel such painful and angry emotions come back to me as I continued to cry and scream loudly. I cried out again and again, "Why? Why did these things happen to me?"

I cried this over and over again with so much passion and emotion and tears still flowing from me. They continued to pray and rebuke the spirit of fear, shame, disappointment, guilt, and anger in my life. After that, they prayed for the Holy Spirit to come and bring healing to me. I could feel such peace come over me. Now I was truly free. Now this wonderful, godly man knelt down in front of me to represent the men who did this to me as a symbol on their behalf and said to me, "Honey, I am sorry for what has happened to you." He asked me to forgive him and all the men for what they had done to me. He asked if he could hug me, and I said yes. I learned that freedom doesn't come because we hide our secrets and put them in a box and try to forget them. Freedom comes when we don't have any more secrets or anything to try to hide any longer. This is when you are really free.

On this same night, another man came forth. He was there with his wife. He had been a missionary for many years and had done many things for the Lord. The Spirit of God had touched him also that night, so much that he also recognized that he needed healing from sexual abuse he had experienced in his life. He cried and cried. Many men have also been sexually abused. We tend to think of this happening to women only.

It was amazing how many people came forth that night. Many people were delivered from many things. I felt very good. It was as though a weight had been lifted from me. I knew I was now free of any strongholds that had once been in my life. We were all very happy about the servants that God had used to help us in our lives. We were all very thankful to God for what had just taken place. This was the end of our three-month course called Cross Road.

We were now planning a two-month missionary trip to Mongolia and New Mexico. The cost would be $3,300. They instructed all of us students to write back to our home churches, our family, and our friends, asking for their support toward this trip. The students all did this, but I couldn't.

There was no one to ask. I hadn't been affiliated with any church in Sweden for a long time, and I didn't want to ask my American friends for more, because they had already been so generous to me. I told the Lord that He was the only one who could get this for me. I wrote a letter to my Daddy God, telling him of my need. I knew He wanted me here and He wanted me to go, so now I would have to trust Him to give me the needed money for my trip. I wrote my letter and put it in my Bible, knowing that my Daddy God would faithfully provide for me.

The very next day, I woke up and went to my class. After we prayed for our trip, the leader asked if the Lord had given any of us a vision or a word about the trip. We were all going together, so he wanted us to share, put it on the chalkboard, and we would be able to find out for what purpose we were going. Many students spoke up and told of visions or words they had from the Lord. I also shared a vision the Lord showed me. In this vision, I saw myself on the streets of Mongolia at a specific place, speaking to two prostitutes. One of my fellow students looked at me—or actually sneered at me—saying, "Oh okay, Sarah, we will see." This student gave me the impression she didn't think I could go on this trip because I didn't have any money.

The next day, I began to experience such kindness from the people at this base. They told me that several people had deposited money into my account equaling the exact amount needed for my trip. My Daddy God had provided once again. I was very excited.

Friday was the last day of our classes, and we had a teacher who taught us about faith. Before the end of the class, our leader came in and made the announcement that everyone needed to have their money for their plane tickets for our missionary trip to Mongolia and New Mexico by Monday. I was very excited that I had my money for the trip. My leader approached me and began to tell me, "Sarah, even if you do have the money, you cannot go with us, because your visa is only good for three months, and there's nothing they could do about it." They were to enforce the immigration laws, which in my case was because I only had a three-month visa and the missionary trip would be for an additional two months. Our missionary trip would begin in New Mexico, which is part of the United States. I understood what he was trying to tell me. I could not remain in the United States longer than three months. I would have to go back to Sweden to get an extension on my visa, and there just was not time to go back to Sweden and then back to Dallas in time to go on this mission trip.

The more we tried to work this out, the more he kept telling me reasons why it would not work. Another couple in our class even made a suggestion that they could drive me over the border from New Mexico to Mexico and then back to New Mexico again. Again, the leader said he could not take the risk, because they told us previously that we would all have to return to our own countries to renew our visas.

I found myself a little bit agitated with his lack of faith, since we had just finished a week of being taught about how we should use our faith. So I said to him, "What are you talking about? You teach us about faith. Are those just words? We have to take action in our faith." He just looked at me, I think a little bit stunned at my response to all he was saying to me.

Then he said, "Okay, Sarah, we cannot take that risk, so the risk is on you. When you go to Mexico, if things do not go as planned, you will have to take responsibility. We cannot."

I said to him, "It is not my risk but the Lord's risk." I went to my room and began to praise the Lord with joy, and I really gave that situation to Him. Then I said, "Lord, I put this matter in your hands."

The time arrived for the trip. All of us were to pack only one small suitcase, a minimal amount for only three weeks. We were to leave all the rest of our belongings at the base. The couple proceeded to take me, as we had planned, to the Mexican border. The police officer at the border checked the couple's passports, and because they were American, they were okay. Even mine was okay, because I also had one week left on visa and my ticket back to Sweden. The police officer said to go, and I said, "No, I cannot go. I need more time on my visa."

He told us to go and park our car and go to the immigration office. I was very thankful to God that he let me go, because they normally only let people go to the immigration office who don't have a visa. We parked our car and went into the immigration office on the border. I went up to the front desk and I said hello to the police officer.

The officer was a little impatient with me; he could not understand why I needed more time, because I still had one more week on my visa. He also questioned my many trips back and forth from Sweden to the United States and back to Sweden. I explained to him that I was a missionary and the Lord had told me to come here. Unkindly, he told me to go sit down. I went and sat down. The couple began to pray, and the officer left the desk.

My memory went back to the vision I shared in the classroom of me in Mongolia, talking to the two prostitutes about Jesus. Another officer approached with a very friendly smile. He said, "What do you want?" Again, I told my story to him. He just looked at me, smiled, and stamped my visa for an additional three months.

I said to him, "Thank you and God bless you." We left quickly because we didn't want to run into the first officer again. What a miracle. We called our fellow students and told them the good news. We were all very excited about what the Lord had done. We were able to put action to our faith, and my Father God, as always, was faithful. I was very blessed.

We got into our car and drove back to the base in New Mexico. On the way, we stopped to celebrate at a really nice restaurant and enjoyed a really good lunch.

We arrived back at the base in New Mexico the same day to celebrate with my fellow students. We spent three weeks in New Mexico, preaching and evangelizing. We painted a school, visited orphanages, visited many poor areas, and shared the gospel. It was a very good experience, and many lives were changed. We drove back to Dallas, spent one night there, and packed again.

In the morning, we got up and then flew to China and from there to Mongolia. It was snowing and very cold. We slept in tents, more nicer than what we were used to; they even had fireplaces in them. We stayed for one month. In that month, we visited jails. In one jail I remember I shared my testimony and Jesus with three men. They accepted Jesus as their Lord and Savior. Some of the students also performed drama. We also met an American missionary named John he had been there for eight years. He has a small place where he and others helped minister to prostitutes and those with drug and alcohol problems. The prostitutes who accepted Jesus and wanted to live their lives for Jesus were allowed to stay there.

Once a week, the prostitutes, along with others from the church, would go out and share the gospel with other prostitutes who were on the streets.

One night, the other students and I went out with this group of prostitutes, and I saw myself exactly as I had seen in my vision in Dallas at the school. I was in the same place, talking to these two prostitutes, and they received Jesus into their hearts. It was amazing and incredible. It was exactly as the Lord showed me.

We visited different cities, helping many people receive Jesus into their hearts. It was an amazing experience. We also visited a local university. We were able to go there because one of the missionary men worked there, so that was our connection to get in. Our purpose was to teach them English for one week. We were instructed that we were not allowed to tell them about Jesus unless they asked us first. Because they were curious about who we were and what we were doing in Mongolia, we found that since they asked, we had many opportunities to share Jesus with the students. Some received Jesus into their hearts. Also, we all spent some time reflecting about all of our experiences and how good it was to learn about other people and their culture.

Now the time had come for us to return to Dallas. We spent one more week in Dallas, having meetings and times of prayer. We talked about our trip and all the good and even some things we could do differently next time.

After that week was over, we came to the end of our course. We would all be returning. The students came from many different states. It was a great experience, but I was very excited to go back home to Sweden to see my children. I had missed them very much.

At the beginning of 2009, the Lord began to speak to me about Honduras. I had a very clear vision at that time as the Lord spoke to me that this was the time I should go to Honduras. I remembered meeting a pastor and his wife from Honduras. I had met them in Ohio about four years ago. I found out the pastor's e-mail address from some friends in Ohio. I sent him an e-mail introducing myself, and shared the vision the Lord gave me with him and his wife about my going to Honduras. The pastor's name was Luis. I asked him to pray and let me know if he felt this was the Lord's timing.

After two weeks, I received an e-mail response from Pastor Luis saying, "Yes, Sister Sarah, you are welcome here, please come."

Now, at this time I had no money for the plane ticket or my living expenses once I was there. So once again I prayed and asked my big Daddy God to provide for his daughter.

Very soon after, my dear sons, with their limited money, presented me with all I needed to fly down to Honduras and be able to pay for my living expenses. This time my Big Daddy provided all I needed through my very favorite people in the world.

Before my trip to Honduras, the Lord put in my heart to ask specific people from the church in Sweden if they would like to bless the Honduran people. I was collecting money to take down to these believers in need. This money was not for any part of my trip, but just for the needy people of Honduras. I collected the little bit of money that was offered.

I left Sweden for Honduras for a three-month stay. When I arrived in Honduras, Pastor Luis and his wife picked me up, and we went to their missionary base, where I settled in.

During the first week, there was another group there at the base, dentists on a medical mission. I got to assist them. I learned so much and helped a lot as we tended to the dental needs of all those kids. It was great. The group was seven dentists and assistants from Oregon. Two dentists were from Honduras. This group from Oregon didn't come from some specific church. They were just with an organization that sends dentists to foreign countries to help out. The group consisted of two Christians, two Mormons, one Muslim, Christians from Pentecostal and Catholic churches, and others who were not believers at all.

During those two weeks, I shared a room with the other ladies from this dental group. We ate together, worked together, slept together, and as we relaxed together in the evening drinking our coffee, I had a chance to share about Jesus's testimony in my life. It was such a great opportunity with such a diverse group. I saw how they were amazed at what the Lord, through His Holy Spirit, did for me. They really listened.

The Mormon dentist started a discussion with me about the Bible, and I prayed, "Please, Holy Spirit, show me what to show him." The Holy Spirit came through for me again as He led me to the exact places in Scripture that answered that Mormon dentist's questions. He didn't continue with his discussion and was quiet and listened. At that moment, I was amazed and blessed at the fact that not only was I able to help these people physically, but also the Lord used me to share Jesus with this mixed group. It felt really good. After two weeks, their time was finished and they returned to the United States.

The next mission group to arrive at our base was also from the United States. They were missionaries from a conservative Christian church. They were here for ten days to help with some construction at the base. Also, they distributed clothes and food and taught the ladies to sew dresses. I also got to help with this group. They had to teach me to sew first; then I taught the ladies. We spent all of our time together with a lot of time for sharing about what Jesus did for us.

I was especially blessed to talk about the Holy Spirit and about how I had never believed in the gift of tongues until one day when it happened to me. I explained about that night I went to a prayer meeting. As the meeting was ending, they called for people who needed prayer to come and sit in front of the group. They began to pray over us. As these people prayed over me, I felt very strongly like hot water was being poured over my head and soaking my clothes.

Then from deep inside, I felt the need to let out some words, but I held my mouth shut very tightly and I didn't want to open it. I didn't want to let those words out, but I felt I couldn't breathe through my nose, so I had to open my mouth. When I did, out came some words that I didn't know. Again I shut my mouth stronger than before, but I had to open it to breathe, and when I did, again out came those words I didn't know. At that moment, I gave up and surrendered to the Lord. I said, "Forgive me, Jesus. Sometimes in our limited thoughts, we limit your Holy Spirit. We try to limit what you want to do in our lives, and we try to tell you in our spirit what is right or wrong."

That night, I was very happy to share this with some Christian people in that group. Maybe some believed in the gift of tongues and maybe some didn't, but it wasn't for me to judge. I got to share from my heart this amazing experience I had with the Holy Spirit.

After ten days, it was time for this group to return. It was such a blessing to be able to work with Christians not just from one building but from the world, the real body of Christ. That was the last large missionary group to come through the base while I was there. After a short time, two people arrived to stay six months at that base. They were a twenty-four-year-old guy and a twenty-year-old girl. The girls stayed in the room with me. The fellow stayed in another room. We really enjoyed our time with each other and with Pastor Luis and his family. As a group, we were able to help another missionary who had an operation in the town. Each Tuesday, early in the morning, we would arrive and pack food up. Then early Wednesday morning, we would take the food up the mountain to share with the people at a house where they would sometimes gather. We got to share the gospel too. With the money I had collected from those people in Sweden, I was able to buy sixty-five pairs of sandals and shoes for the women and children on that mountain who needed them. The Lord put in my heart to talk with Pastor Luis about having a three-day women's conference. He agreed. It was amazing. I spoke and taught out of the Bible about many things.

On the third day, near the end of the meeting, the Lord told me, "Now ask the women who have been molested or abused or raped to come forward for prayer." I did ask them. I said, "The Lord says there is among you some who have been molested, abused, or raped. The Lord wants to deliver you and heal your pain." I invited them to come. No one came forward. Inside me, I said, "Lord, why did you tell me to ask them for this? Look, no one is coming forward, and I feel embarrassed!"

Suddenly, I felt the Holy Spirit tell me, "No, they aren't coming forward, so I will show you who they are, and you will go to them." I asked my Spanish translator to follow me as I went up to the first woman the Holy Spirit showed me. I whispered in her ear, "The Lord showed me that you were sexually abused as a child. Is it true? Just tell me. If it is, I want to pray for you in private after the meeting." She said yes and began to shake and cry. Then the Lord showed me the next one, then the next one, then the next, and the cases were different, but of about 150 ladies, He led me right to the very ones who needed His touch.

After the meeting, I prayed for them as they told me one by one in private that this was the first time they had spoken to anyone about this. I knew that God knew their secret. We prayed, and those precious women received real healing that day as we gave thanks for our Heavenly Father and praised the name of Jesus and glory to His name. He even gave me a hard word for one married woman there. He showed me that she was having an affair and the Lord wanted her to turn from that sin. He asked me to tell her this message in private. My heart was beating fast as I approached her. I didn't want to say this hard word to her. But I had to obey my wonderful faithful Daddy. I went to her and told her what the Lord had showed me. I said, "You think nobody knows about your secret affair, but the Lord, the Holy One and Mighty One sees you. He knows about your affair and he wants you to turn away from it now or you will have to face the consequence." The lady's face turned red and she was totally silent. She couldn't deny it.

After the conference, I was very thankful to God for what He did. He touched many lives. I wanted to stay in Honduras for three months. Three weeks before I was scheduled to return, I was fasting and praying as I sat on the front porch of the mission house. I was wondering and asking the Lord, "What is next for me?" A Honduran girl had arrived at the base that day, and as I was sitting there, she passed by me on that porch. She looked over at me and said, "Oh, excuse me, I don't know why, but the Lord just told me, and I want to tell you that you should write about your life."

I looked over at her. She looked at me and just walked away. My thoughts went back over my years of following Jesus. When I shared these things about my life people would often ask me, "Why don't you write about your life?" I would always say, "No, no, no." I didn't want to write about my life. I never had the desire in my heart to do that. I never gave it another thought when they suggested it. Now, after this girl had said the exact thing to me, and after all these years of ignoring the suggestion, I couldn't get it out of my head. I asked God, "What's wrong with me, Lord? Why can't I forget about this?"

He spoke to my heart. "Sarah, this time it's me, and I want you to write about your life." I asked Him about this request. "How, Lord? I have no money, no desire in my heart to do this, and I don't even know where to start. I speak Persian, Swedish, and English. What language do you want me to write this book in? How do I do something like this? If it's you, Lord, give me the desire and a clear picture about how to do this."

I sat and prayed and said nothing to anyone about this thing. That night, I had a very, very clear and strong dream. It was very real. In my dream, there was an open place, like a huge open field. The field was filled with many children. They were black and white children all sitting together cross-legged in that field. I was sitting cross-legged in front of that group of children. I was facing President Obama, who was sitting cross-legged on the ground face-to-face with me. In the dream, I became able to share with President Obama about my life from the time I was a child, as the children listened from behind.

As I spoke, starting from my childhood experiences, a flock of blackbirds began to rise in the air between us. They rose into the air, but it seemed they couldn't get very high for some reason. Then suddenly a flock of white doves began to rise up from the ground between the president and me, and as they rose higher and higher, they scattered the blackbirds away. I didn't see them anymore, but the white doves continued to rise up, up into the air. They filled the sky and flew out in all different directions from that place. When I woke up, I felt that dream was 100 percent from the Lord. I was sure it was the Lord who spoke to me. I knew it in my spirit and mind and heart.

Early that morning, I got up to walk and pray. I told the Lord that I knew He sent me that dream and I asked Him, "What does this dream from you mean?" The Lord began to speak to me. "Remember yesterday, Sarah, when you asked me where to start, and how to start, and what language to start this book? In your dream, you saw President Obama, and he represents to you the country of the United States. The black and white children represent to you the people of the United States. The blackbirds represent all the difficult and painful trials in your life. The white doves represent the Holy Spirit. In the dream, when you began to share about your life, this represents my will that you write a book about your life from your childhood until now. Also, you saw the white doves that rose up and scattered the blackbirds away. This represents the Holy Spirit, who pushes away the pain and darkness from your life and brings deliverance and healing. You saw that the white doves went very high and flew off in all different directions. This represents the book will move out into many cities in the United States, because Sarah, what I did for you, I desire to do for many people who believe I can do this for them too."

I was very excited and shocked at what the Lord had shown me. I said, "Okay, Lord, what city do you want me to start from? Who do you want me to ask for help? Lord, you know I can't write very well in English." He told me to ask Pastor Chuck in Ohio. The Lord said, "You talk to him and he will help you."

"Okay, I will ask him. Now, Lord, where shall I stay?" I asked him and he said, "Ken and Mary's home, the people you know from four years ago." I asked him how I will actually write this book in English. He said to me, "Don't worry, Sarah, I will bring people to you. Some people who can write this in English for you while you tell your life story to them and drink your coffee."

After I finished talking over the details with my Daddy God, I returned to my room and sat on my bed and pondered all this in my heart.

The days passed quickly, and the time came for me to return to Sweden. My sons picked me up at the airport, and I was overjoyed to see them and their beautiful faces. After I settled in, I began to enjoy the time together with my children as we talked about many things. I shared with them about the vision the Lord gave me to write about my life. They were excited about what the Lord had done in my life and about what he planned to do through my life for others. The next step was to contact Pastor Chuck in Ohio, to share this vision with him. I e-mailed him and told him everything about the dream and how the Lord translated it for me. I told him, "Pastor Chuck, I know you have such a nice heart and you are a gentleman. Please pray about this and let me know if you really feel that this is from the Lord."

About three weeks later, I received an e-mail from Pastor Chuck, and he said he felt that this was from the Lord and for me to come here and he would help me. My next step was to contact Mary and Ken. I met this wonderful family in 2005 when I was in Ohio for three months. They asked me to stay with them, and we grew very close during this time. Their love and friendship and hospitality made me feel very welcome in their home. Mary became like a sister to me and Ken like a brother. They, along with their wonderful children, make me feel like family. I called Mary and told her about my vision. It was amazing because Mary told me that three weeks ago when she was at the church talking to Pastor Chuck, she told him that she felt in her heart that she wanted to invite me to stay with her for a while. Pastor Chuck said to Mary, "Guess what, I received an e-mail from Sarah about her vision to come to America and write a book about her life." It was amazing that the time Mary wanted to invite me was the same time I e-mailed Pastor Chuck to come to America. It made me very glad to hear this, because before I even needed to ask to stay with her, the Lord had already provided a place for me.

I arrived in the United States October 19, 2009. I stayed with this wonderful family, and my God provided some wonderful Christian women to help me as I share my testimony, to write it down for me. I pray to God that He bless them for everything they do in His name.

I would like to give you a brief explanation of my children's lives right now. My eldest son Cyrus, who lived a 100 percent worldly life and did not believe in Jesus, has now received Jesus as his Lord and Savior, and now his life has been totally transformed from worldly living to living his life for Christ. He has in his heart in the future to be a successful businessman and use his money for God's kingdom. He has a very tender, gentle, giving, and wonderful heart. He says to me, "Mom, what right choices I used to make were because of you, but now they are because of Jesus."

My second son Kevin, who was very wild and worldly, is the one I have called "the storm." He was the one who criticized my faith in Jesus the most. He has also accepted Jesus into his heart, and his life has been completely transformed and delivered from drug addiction. He is married to a wonderful and beautiful born-again Christian woman named Mariëlla. Kevin and Mariëlla have a calling from the Lord as evangelists and missionaries. They travel extensively to many countries, sharing the gospel with many people. I don't call him "the storm" any longer; I call him "fire for the Lord."

My youngest son Alex, when I talked to him about God, used to say, "Mom, when I get old, then I'll think about God." He has also accepted the Lord Jesus into his heart, and Jesus has completely changed his life. He now says to me, "Mom, Christianity is not a religion, but Christianity is a lifestyle." He was a professional kickboxer. He was a twice champion in Sweden and once in Scandinavia. He was third out of sixty-eight countries. He left the sport to fulfill the call of God on his life as a pastor. He is planning to attend Bible college in the near future.

You can see the Lord has healed our lives of much pain and sorrow and delivered us from a lot of darkness. I feel a desire in my heart that in the future, I would like to write another book about the specific details of my children's lives. From the time before they knew Jesus until now has been a long process, and many things happened to bring them to where they are now. I just want you to know that the Lord has healed us and can do the same for you and your family.

Now, my wonderful reader, I want to tell you in general what is going on in my life situation and about the desire in my heart for the future.

During the seven years from 2003 to 2010, I traveled to many countries to talk about Jesus and help the needy. It was all of the Lord's grace. Some of the countries I mentioned and some I did not, for certain safety reasons. Forgive me. I want to tell you a short statement about my personal feelings. Now I know I am Cinderella and my beautiful Daddy God is the King. My Prince Charming came into my life and rescued me with His true love, and His name is Jesus. I have the best Friend in the whole world, and His Name is the dear Holy Spirit. I realize I am still single, but I know the Lord didn't call me to stay this way. I know some day my Daddy God will bring to me a true believer. He will bring me someone He can trust as a husband for His daughter.

Now to let you know about my living situation: During those seven years that I traveled, I sold everything I had and went out with no income, no car, no home, and no property anywhere in this world. I lived wherever the Lord opened a door for me. I trusted God and lived by faith for each day. He provided for me. Today I'm still living by faith for provision for each day. I still have no income, no car, no home, and no property anywhere in the world, but I feel in my heart that this year, in the year 2010, after all those years of traveling and living in many people's homes, now the Lord wants to settle me in one country. Then He will send me out from that place as He calls me as His evangelist.

He has given me a special and strong desire in my heart to set up bases in different poor countries where women and children have been sexually and physically abused in their homes, for women who have no one to protect them and women with so much pain and sorrow in their heart and in their souls. This would be a place to take care of them and teach them that they are important and wonderful. There is someone who loves them and wants to take care of them, and His name is Abba Father. He wants to do this through His people, through His body in Christ. He wants to help them and deliver them from that pain and darkness so they can be someone in this life who can help others, wherever they are in this world.

Before I end, I want to tell you now, it doesn't matter what is going on in your life or your family. God wants to deliver you and heal you and set you free and give you eternal life. If you open up your heart and choose to want to help, I know God is able to restore hope, joy, purpose, and deliver you from whatever is holding you captive. No matter what your circumstances, I know this, because God our Heavenly Father, through His Son Jesus and His Holy Spirit has done this for us.

May God bless you forever!

Sarah,
Servant of the Lord Jesus

LaVergne, TN USA
22 January 2011
213563LV00004B/1/P